# Seasonal SPECIALS for Children's Ministry

Children's group ACTIVITIES for **ten**
**key occasions** through the year

Barnabas for Children® is a registered word mark and the logo is a registered device mark of
The Bible Reading Fellowship.

**The Bible Reading Fellowship**
15 The Chambers, Vineyard
Abingdon OX14 3FE
brf.org.uk

BRF is a Registered Charity (233280)

ISBN 978 0 85746 525 2
First UK edition published 2016
10 9 8 7 6 5 4 3 2 1 0
All rights reserved

Illustrations by Kate Elvin, Mernie Gallagher-Cole (Portfolio Solutions, LLC), RoseAnne Sather, Rebecca Swain

Originally published in the USA
by Group Publishing, Inc. under the title
*Seasonal Specials for Children's Ministry: All-New Ideas for 13 Holidays*
Copyright © 2012 by Group Publishing, Inc.

**Acknowledgements**
Scripture quotations are taken from the Holy Bible, New Living Translation, copyright © 1996, 2004, 2007, 2013.
Used by permission of Tyndale House Publishers, Inc., Carol Stream, Illinois 60188. All rights reserved.

Every effort has been made to trace and contact copyright owners for material used in this resource. We apologise
for any inadvertent omissions or errors, and would ask those concerned to contact us so that full acknowledgement
can be made in the future.

A catalogue record for this book is available from the British Library

Printed by Gutenberg Press, Tarxien, Malta

# Contents

## MOTHER'S DAY

## FATHER'S DAY

## HARVEST

## HALLOWEEN

## REMEMBRANCE DAY

## CHRISTMAS

# Introduction

**S**unday morning often revolves around what's happening during the year. If children are decorating red hearts with 1 Corinthians 13:13 stickers, Valentine's Day is probably around the corner. Painting a flowerpot? It must be Mother's Day. And for those who minister to children, these special occasions can be the hardest times to find fresh, faith-focused ideas.

That's where *Seasonal Specials for Children's Ministry* comes in.

We've planned celebrations for ten popular occasions—all from a Christian perspective. Whether you're leading preschool children or preteens, you can have fun with a Bible focus, a craft, a game, a snack, a drama sketch, a song and an outreach idea. That means right now you're holding more than 70 innovative and engaging ideas to ensure that these occasions will be more than just a highlighted date on a calendar. Instead, they'll be Jesus-centred experiences.

This book covers major celebrations (Easter, Christmas and New Year's Day) as well as other events such as Valentine's Day, Harvest, Halloween and Remembrance Day. Each section has fresh ideas that inspire, educate and celebrate.

You'll find the events arranged chronologically, so finding exactly what you're looking for is simple. You can use an entire section as a full session, or simply pick and choose elements to add to a session. Here's an example of the elements you'll find in each chapter.

## NEW YEAR'S DAY

**Pressing on** (Bible focus)
**New Year's crackers** (craft)
**Second chance** (game)
**New life gingerbread people** (snack)
**A clean heart** (sketch)
**Jesus makes all of us new** (song)
**Book beginnings** (outreach)

Each element includes a Bible reading, age recommendations, a list of supplies needed, easy-to-follow instructions and thoughtful questions aimed at helping children explore what they experience.

Jesus used what was around him to teach people about God—including daily life and seasons. He told parables about the harvest, fig trees and mustard seeds, all in conjunction with what was happening on the calendar. *Seasonal Specials for Children's Ministry* is designed to follow that model, making our annual celebrations both memorable and meaningful.

Be aware that some children have food allergies that can be dangerous. Know the children in your group, and consult with parents about allergies their children may have. Read food labels carefully, as hidden ingredients can cause allergy-related problems. Look for the Allergy Alert symbol against certain activities.

Please follow your church's safeguarding policy at all times, and secure parental permission for all relevant activities, for example when taking children offsite.

# New Year's Day

New Year's Day... new beginnings... a collective second chance. It's the time of year for genuine reflection, slate-wiping and (soon-to-be-forgotten?!) New Year's resolutions. As you celebrate a new year, children will discover how, through Jesus, they're new creations—blank canvases, ready for God to paint some love on their hearts.

# Pressing on

BEST
Primary Age
FOR

*Children are encouraged to move on from the past and press forward for Jesus!*

### SCRIPTURE

Philippians 3:13–14

### WHAT YOU'LL NEED

• Bible
• sign with last year's date on it
• sign with this year's date on it
• Blu-Tack® or similar

## The experience

Hang your signs on opposite walls, and clear the area between the walls of any obstacles.

Ask the children to face last year's sign.

SAY: **Let's reflect on the past year. Raise your hand if you've done what I call out.**

  • **Who visited a different country last year?**
  • **Who got a new brother or sister last year?**
  • **Who did something you were proud of?**
  • **Who did something you regret?**

SAY: **We've all done things we regret. Maybe we did something embarrassing, or maybe we really hurt someone by our actions. Sometimes the memories of those regrets stick in our minds and make us feel bad. Getting stuck on what we did in the past can really mess up how we feel about the future. I'll show you what I mean.**

Ask the children to continue facing last year's wall and to walk until they're standing right up against it.

SAY: **Your goal is to race across the room, but you have to walk backwards, keeping your eyes on last year. If you bump into anyone or fall down or peek behind you, you have to sit right where you are, so be careful!**

Allow a few minutes for the children to do this. Declare the winner and then ask the children to sit in a circle.

ASK: **What was hard about racing backwards?**

• **Talk about a time when you focused on a mistake or bad choice you made—and it caused a problem for you.**

• **How can remembering our bad choices help or hurt our future?**

SAY: **It's good to learn from the things we've done wrong. But when we hold on to guilt or bad feelings, we forget that God has forgiven us. We can get stuck in the past, thinking God doesn't love us any more. But the Bible has something important to say about holding on to the past as we go through life.**

Read Philippians 3:13–14.

Get the children to go back to last year's wall.

SAY: **Let's put this verse into practice. Rather than focusing on what's behind us (last year), let's look towards what's ahead. Turn around and race to the sign for the new year. Ready? Go!**

When all the children are at the new sign, declare them all winners.

ASK: **What does it mean to 'press on' for God?**

• **How can you live for Jesus this year?**

SAY: **A lot of people make resolutions on New Year's Day. We vow to do things such as get more exercise, read more or eat healthier foods. Those are all good goals. But the most important goal we have is a lifelong one: to live for Jesus. If we live every day with our eyes focused on him, we'll have fewer regrets each year. And we'll also know that Jesus forgives us for the wrong things we do when we ask him to. So don't dwell in the past—just keep your eyes on what Jesus has in store for you this year!**

# Craft

# New Year's Eve crackers

**BEST** **All Ages** **FOR**

*Children make a New Year's Eve craft as a reminder to live for Jesus in the new year.*

## Scripture

Ephesians 5:15–16a

## What you'll need

- Bible
- kitchen towel tubes or wrapping paper tubes cut to 21 cm
- colourful paper
- metallic pens
- safety scissors
- colourful tissue paper
- metallic curling ribbon
- wrapped sweets
- clear sticky tape
- shiny stickers

## The experience

Before the children arrive, cut some of the tissue paper into rectangles around 19 cm wide and 42 cm long (big enough to wrap the tubes and leave some tissue paper to tie at each end). Cut metallic curling ribbon into 30 cm lengths. Cut colourful paper into 3 cm x 10 cm strips. For younger children, write or print the words from Ephesians 5:15–16a on the strips of paper.

SAY: **Happy New Year! People around the globe celebrate the arrival of a new year with lots of traditions.**

ASK: **What New Year's Eve traditions does your family have?**

SAY: **Today we're going to make party crackers to celebrate the new year. We're going to put treats and a paper crown into the crackers, but we're also going to include an important message about how to live for Jesus in the coming year.**

**First, we'll work on our**

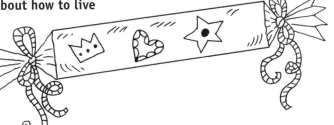

**message. There's a great Bible verse that can help us know how to live for Jesus this year.**

Read aloud Ephesians 5:15–16a. Pass out the slips of colourful paper and help the children each write this verse on a slip using the metallic pens. Then get them to tuck the paper in their kitchen towel tube.

ASK: **What do you think this verse means?**

- **What does it mean to 'make the most of every opportunity'?**

SAY: **Now let's make a paper crown to tuck inside the cracker. Our crowns can remind us that when Jesus is king of our lives, we live for him.**

Show the children how to cut out a piece of tissue paper that will fit around their heads with a few extra centimetres left to overlap and tape. They can cut zig-zags along the top to look more crown-like. When they've finished, get them to gently fold the hats to fit into the tubes.

Help the children to wrap their tubes with tissue paper and tie one end with curling ribbon. Then get them to put some sweets in the tubes along with the paper slips and crowns before tying the other end with ribbon. (For younger children, choose sweets that aren't choking hazards.) The children can decorate the outside of the tubes with metallic pens or stickers.

SAY: **Take your party cracker home with you. As you celebrate the new year, crack it open. Read the verse and enjoy the sweets with your family as you pray for God's help in making the most of every opportunity in the coming year.**

# Game

# Second chance

*Children either get a second chance or they don't when aiming paper aeroplanes at a target.*

**SCRIPTURE**

2 Corinthians 5:17

**WHAT YOU'LL NEED**

- Bible
- sheets of paper
- masking tape

## The experience

Give each child a sheet of paper to fold into a paper aeroplane. (For younger children, demonstrate how to make a paper plane or let them just crumple their paper and throw it like a ball.) Once the children have created their planes, use masking tape to make a square target on the floor a metre or so away.

SAY: **The goal of this game is to land your plane or ball inside the square.**

Without allowing any time to practise, let the children take turns trying to land their plane or ball inside the tape square. If the child misses the square but the plane lands right side up, say, 'Second chance!' and let them try again until they hit the target or the plane lands upside down. (If children are throwing balls, give a second chance to every other child who misses.) If a child's plane lands upside down, that child doesn't get another chance. However, don't explain *why* certain children get a second chance and others don't until the end of the game. Note: children may get frustrated that some people get a second chance and others don't; that's OK—it's part of the experience. If you have time, play again.

ASK: **What does it mean to get a second chance?**

• **How did you react when you either got or didn't get a second chance in this game?**

• **Talk about a time someone gave you a second chance in your life.**

• **If you could have one second chance in real life, what would you do again, and why?**

SAY: **The new year is a time to remember the past and look forward to the future. It's a fresh start and a second chance to do properly the things we've messed up. God offered us the biggest second chance ever when he sent Jesus. Because Jesus died for us, we get a second chance. In 2 Corinthians 5:17, the Bible says that anyone who belongs to Christ has become a new person. Out with the old, and in with the new! Our sins are wiped away, like wiping clean a blackboard. We can start afresh. Let's fly into the new year thanking God for giving us a second chance.**

# New life gingerbread people

*Children discover that no matter how messy life gets, they get a new start with Jesus.*

**SCRIPTURE**

2 Corinthians 5:17

**WHAT YOU'LL NEED**

- Bible
- 1 gingerbread person per child
- paper plates
- plastic knives
- white icing
- strawberry laces
- Smarties® or yogurt-covered raisins
- plastic spoons
- yellow fondant icing rolled into small cones, to look like bugles (optional)

## The experience

Ask the children to wash their hands, then give each child a gingerbread person on a paper plate, with the top side of the gingerbread person facing downwards. Set out the supplies (except the yellow fondant bugles).

SAY: **Use the supplies to decorate your gingerbread person. But you have to do it with your eyes closed.**

Allow time; then tell the children to open their eyes.

ASK: **What do you think of your gingerbread creation?**

• **How does a messy gingerbread person remind you of what we feel like when we've done something wrong?**

SAY: **The Bible says we've all done wrong things. On the inside, we've all looked like a messy gingerbread person. But listen to this!**

Read aloud 2 Corinthians 5:17.

SAY: **Let's make our gingerbread people into new people, just like Jesus did for us. As we start this new year, we can celebrate our new life in Jesus.**

Get the children to scrape off their icing and decorations and then turn over the gingerbread person so it is facing up the right way. Then let the children keep their eyes open and redecorate their gingerbread people.

Optional: ask the children to put a fondant bugle in the gingerbread person's mouth to remind them to celebrate new life in Jesus.

Then let them eat their gingerbread people.

ASK: **How will you live life differently this year knowing that Jesus made you a new person?**

SAY: **All we need to do is ask, and we'll belong to Jesus. That means we're new people! Remembering what Jesus has done for us can help us remember to live like we're new this year.**

# A clean heart

*Kate learns how God gets rid of sin.*

### SCRIPTURE

Psalm 51:10

### PROPS

- chair
- stethoscope (toy or real)
- large ball
- black tape

### CAST

- Jesus
- Kate

### BEHIND THE SCENES

This is a simple set-up with just a chair for Kate, on one side of the stage. Kate holds a ball with two black strips of tape stuck to it. Jesus wears a stethoscope.

 **Action!**

➡ *Kate sits in the chair. She's waiting, and has a large ball covered with strips of black tape in her hands. Jesus enters with a stethoscope around his neck.*

### JESUS

OK... Kate? Is Kate out here?

### KATE

That's me.

### JESUS

You're up next!

---

My notes say you have questions about your heart.

➡ *Kate stands. She starts to hold out her ball with the black tape on it, but she pulls back. She's a bit hesitant.*

### KATE

Yes, but... I'm not sure what's going to happen.

### JESUS

Oh?

➡ *Kate looks at the ball.*

### KATE

My mum says God looks at our hearts. And I'm not so sure mine is OK. She says he forgives us if we do something wrong—just wipes our heart clean.

### JESUS

Right. Your mum's a smart cookie.

### KATE

But I don't get it.

### JESUS

It's just like she says. Wiped clean. A second chance. Like New Year's Day, new year, new things, starting again...

 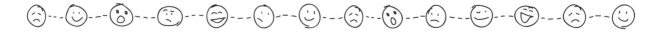

**KATE**

So, if I do something wrong, and I ask God to forgive me, then that thing I did just... goes away?

**JESUS**

Well, yes. He forgives you. Gone. Adios.

➡ *Kate hands the ball to Jesus.*

**KATE**

Will it hurt?

➡ *Jesus smiles, reassuring Kate.*

**JESUS**

It might. There might be things you don't want to admit or don't want to talk about. Are you ready?

➡ *Kate looks at Jesus as if to say, 'Do I have to?' Jesus nods and smiles. He points to a specific piece of black tape.*

**JESUS**

Let's start here. What's this one?

**KATE**

*(Hesitantly)* I lied to my mum.

**JESUS**

Oooh. Not the best idea. Hold still.

➡ *Kate stands completely still, eyes shut in a wince, as if waiting for something to hurt. Jesus pulls off the tape in one swift motion, as if quickly pulling off a plaster. Kate slowly peeks out of one eye at Jesus.*

**KATE**

That... wasn't that bad.

**JESUS**

Great! But... that's not all of it. Your heart still looks like this. *(Points to another piece)* What about this one?

**KATE**

That one I don't really want to talk about. It's going to hurt.

**JESUS**

God wants to help you with everything, Kate. Even the hard stuff.

**KATE**

Well, I'm not forgiving him! He did it on purpose!

**JESUS**

If you don't forgive your brother, then God can't forgive you.

**KATE**

But he hurt my feelings! He made fun of me in front of my friends!

**JESUS**

I know it's hard. Maybe you want to get back at him. But that's not how God does things.

**KATE**

But my brother was wrong!

**JESUS**

And you still need to forgive him. *(Pauses)* **Are you ready?**

➡ *Kate gives a big sigh. She looks at Jesus.*

**JESUS**

Remember, it'll be like New Year's Day every day.

**KATE**

*(Grimacing)* **New Year's Day every day...**

**JESUS**

Fresh start. Clean heart. Just like New Year's Day. Ready?

**KATE**

Ready.

➡ *Jesus pulls off the piece of black tape. Kate winces, but then breathes more easily.*

**KATE**

Wow. I feel a lot better. You were right. Thanks.

➡ *Kate turns and starts to leave.*

**JESUS**

I'll be here to help whenever you need me. Oh, Kate?

**KATE**

Yes?

**JESUS**

Here's your heart back. Good as new.

➡ *Jesus hands Kate the ball. Both smile.*

# Jesus makes all of us new

BEST
Preschool
FOR

*Children dance and sing as they give everything to Jesus, to the tune of the 'Mexican hat dance'. (Clips are available on YouTube if you don't know the tune.)*

**SCRIPTURE**

2 Corinthians 5:17

## Sing it!

**When we give all our heart to**
 *(children jump and shout)* **Jesus!**
**When we give all our mind to**
 *(children jump and shout)* **Jesus!**
**When we give all our soul to**
 *(children jump and shout)* **Jesus!**
**Jesus makes all of us new!**

**And then Jesus will give you a new life,**
 *(children do-si-do around each other)*
**And then Jesus will give you a new life,**
 *(children do-si-do around each other)*
**And then Jesus will give you a new life,**
 *(children do-si-do around each other)*
**Jesus makes all of us new!** *(children throw arms up in air)*

# Book beginnings

**BEST Primary Age FOR**

*Books will get a new lease of life as children replace damaged covers.*

### SCRIPTURE

Isaiah 43:18–19

### WHAT YOU'LL NEED

- Bible
- clear sticky tape
- parcel paper or wrapping paper
- scissors
- staplers (use only with adult supervision)
- cotton buds
- rubber bands
- glue
- felt-tip pens and crayons
- stickers
- clear self-adhesive covering film

## The experience

In early December, publicise your need for donations of worn and used children's books. Set up a box at church or school (with the school's permission) to collect the books. Establish a cut-off date for donations a week before you intend to make repairs to the books. Also, find a children's reading group in your community. Many communities have schemes through libraries, schools or charitable organisations to help children practise reading.

Sort the books by the repair they need—such as torn covers, loose spines and so on.

Sit in a circle and <u>SAY:</u> **A new year means new beginnings—a great time for a fresh start! Here's what God has to say about new beginnings.** Read Isaiah 43:18–19. **Today we're going to give some books new beginnings. We'll repair their covers, and then find new homes for them.**

Divide tasks, according to age group if necessary. Repair the books as needed.

Loose pages, depending on the type of book, can be reattached by stapling, taping or glueing. When using glue to reattach pages or covers, use cotton buds for tight places, such as bindings. Then wrap rubber bands around the books and let them sit overnight.

For torn covers, let the children have fun decorating their own replacement covers using the parcel paper or wrapping paper. Follow these steps for making new covers for books.

**1.** Roll out a large piece of parcel paper or wrapping paper and lay it flat.

**2.** Choose a book and lay it in the centre of the paper. Fold the bottom up to meet the edge of the book, and crease the paper. Repeat at the top. Remove the book and finish the fold so you have two pieces the length of the paper folded over at the top and the bottom.

**3.** Place the book in the centre of the paper, on top of the folds, and position it until the left and right sides appear to be equal. Fold the paper over the front cover from the left side.

**4.** Fold this paper inside the front cover. If the paper is too long, trim so it covers about three-quarters of the inside cover. Insert the cover into the flap made by the folds. Close and pull the paper tightly around the front cover.

**5.** Fold the right side of the paper inside the back cover. Trim if necessary. Insert the back cover into the flap.

**6.** Decorate the outside with felt-tip pens, crayons and stickers. Don't forget to include the title of the book and the author! Reinforce the cover with clear self-adhesive covering film.

Donate the repaired books to a children's reading group, or if they don't need them, ask the children to take them home and give them to a friend.

## Extra-special FACTS

### DID YOU KNOW...?

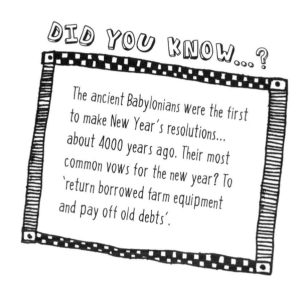

The ancient Babylonians were the first to make New Year's resolutions... about 4000 years ago. Their most common vows for the new year? To 'return borrowed farm equipment and pay off old debts'.

### DID YOU KNOW...?

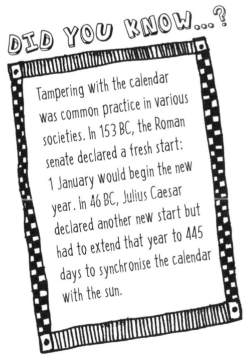

Tampering with the calendar was common practice in various societies. In 153 BC, the Roman senate declared a fresh start: 1 January would begin the new year. In 46 BC, Julius Caesar declared another new start but had to extend that year to 445 days to synchronise the calendar with the sun.

Heart-shaped chocolate boxes and pink teddy bears fill the shops at this time of year, as romance flourishes through gift-giving and odes of affection. But there's a love much greater than romantic love between valentines: God's unconditional, eternal love. And best of all, God extends his love to everyone. As you celebrate Valentine's Day, help children to celebrate the greatest love of all... and learn how they can share God's message with others.

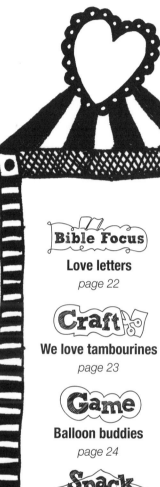

# Love letters

*Children dig into God's sweet love for them and can offer their love in return.*

## SCRIPTURE

1 John 4:7–12

## WHAT YOU'LL NEED

- Bible
- large bowl
- heart-shaped sweets or chocolates
- sheets of white card
- felt-tip pens

## The experience

Ask the children to wash their hands.

SAY: **Valentine's Day is a special day when we can tell others how much we love and appreciate them. We might do this by sending our friends cards, giving people chocolates or telling others how we feel about them. Let's see what the Bible says about expressing our love for others.**

Get the children to form a circle. Pour the heart-shaped chocolates or sweets into a large bowl and place it in the centre of the circle (depending on the number of children present, you may need more than one bowl). Explain to the children that every time they hear the words *love, loves* or *loved* in the passage, each child can take one heart from the bowl.

Read aloud 1 John 4:7–12, pausing to allow the children time to take a heart. When you've finished reading the passage, each child should have 13 hearts.

SAY: **Eat one heart and talk about a time you needed God's love.**

- **Eat another heart, and talk about how God has shown his love for you.**

- **What do these verses teach us about** *real* **love?**

SAY: **On Valentine's Day we focus on loving others. It's important that we express our love for others; that pleases God. Most importantly, we want to show our love for the One who loves us most—God. He shows us his love in so many ways. So let's create a Valentine's Day card to tell God how we feel about him.**

Give each child a sheet of card. Ask them to fold the sheet in half to create a card. Then encourage them to write a love letter to God and to decorate it with felt-tip pens.

Once the children have each completed a love letter, encourage them to read theirs aloud to the group. Then everyone can enjoy some more sweets as you discuss the following question.

ASK: **What are some ways you can show your love for God this week?**

SAY: **Just as you expressed your love for God in a letter, God tells us how he feels about us in his love letter, the Bible. That's where we can read about how he showed his love for us by sending Jesus to take the punishment for our sins. This Valentine's Day, let's celebrate God's love by remembering what he's done for us and by loving those around us.**

# We love tambourines

**BEST** / **All Ages** / **FOR**

*Children make tambourines to celebrate that God's faithful love endures forever.*

**SCRIPTURE**

Psalm 136:1–3

**WHAT YOU'LL NEED**

- Bible
- paper plates, 2 per child
- jingle bells
- small, solid objects such as beads, buttons or bottle tops
- staplers (adult supervision needed)
- hole punches
- wool
- felt-tip pens or crayons
- scraps of pink, purple and red tissue paper
- Mod Podge® sealer
- paintbrushes

## The experience

Read aloud Psalm 136:1–3.

<u>SAY:</u> **This psalm praises God and thanks him for all he's done to show his love. We're going to celebrate what God has done to show love to us. But first, we need some rhythm!**

Hand out two paper plates per child. Help the children to staple the plates together around the edges, about 2.5 cm from the edge, leaving a small opening at the top. Pour about a quarter of a cup of beads, buttons or bottle tops into each pair of plates (make sure younger children don't put the objects in their mouths), and then help the children to staple the hole shut.

Use a hole punch to make three holes around the edges of the plates, outside the stapled circles. Get the children to tie a piece of wool through each hole and attach jingle bells.

For younger children, draw a large heart on each side of the plate, and encourage them to colour their hearts with felt-tip pens or crayons. Ask older children to draw hearts and then use a paintbrush to fill in the hearts with Mod Podge® sealer. Let the children arrange scraps of tissue paper on the sealer to create a stained-glass look. When they've finished adding tissue paper, they'll need to apply another layer of Mod Podge® sealer.

Ask the children to stand in a circle.

<u>SAY:</u> **Now let's make up our own praise chant like the one in Psalm 136. We'll go around the circle and each person can say one thing they're thankful for. When it's your turn, shake your tambourine while you say what you're thankful for. Then we'll all shake our tambourines and say, 'His faithful love endures forever!'**

Go around the circle once; then let the children add extra things they're thankful for.

# Balloon buddies

BEST Primary Age FOR

*Children try not to 'let down' their buddies in this hands-off, high-energy game.*

## SCRIPTURE

Psalm 36:5–9

## WHAT YOU'LL NEED

- Bible
- 1 balloon per person
- permanent markers
- large bin bag

ALLERGY ALERT *See p. 7*

## The experience

Hand each child a balloon, and ask them to inflate and tie their balloons (younger children will need an adult to do this). Let each person draw a simple face on his or her balloon using the permanent markers (supervise younger children so no pen gets on their clothes). Then gather the balloons into a large bin bag.

Ask the children to link arms to make a circle. Hold up one balloon, and SAY: **In this game, we'll see how long we can keep our friend here off the ground. If you let this balloon buddy touch the ground, we'll have to start again.**

Explain that the children can use their heads, knees, bodies or feet to keep the balloon off the ground—but they can't use their hands (since their arms are linked). Throw the balloon into the middle of the circle to start the game. After 30 seconds, SAY: **Let's add a little more challenge.** Add a second balloon and play again.

After another 30 seconds, SAY: **OK, now I know you're ready for a *big* challenge.** Throw all the balloons in the middle of the circle and see if the children can keep them off the ground. Allow 60 chaotic seconds as the children try to keep the balloons off the ground. (Ensure that no one gets kicked in the process.)

Then collect the balloons, and ASK:

- **On a scale of 1 to 5—with 1 being lousy and 5 being perfect—how good were you at keeping our balloon buddies off the ground? Why did you rate yourself that way?**
- **What was hard about keeping the balloons in the air?**

SAY: **Sometimes in real life, people let us down. People might break promises or forget to do something. Find a partner, and talk about a time someone disappointed you or let you down.**

Allow a few minutes for the children to share their experiences.

Read aloud Psalm 36:5–9, and ASK:

- **What does 'unfailing love' mean to you?**
- **How would you show someone else unfailing love?**
- **What is one example of God's unfailing love in *your* life?**

SAY: **In our game, we let the balloon people down—literally! But God's love never fails; he never lets us down. God holds each of us tenderly and lovingly in his arms always, no matter what. This Valentine's Day, let's celebrate God's love.**

Warning! To avoid choking hazards, be sure to pick up pieces of any broken balloons promptly. Balloons may contain latex.

# Blackcurrant surprise

BEST
All Ages
FOR

*This fizzy drink is bursting with Valentine's Day love.*

### SCRIPTURE

1 Thessalonians 3:12

### WHAT YOU'LL NEED

- Bible
- vanilla ice cream
- sparkling water
- blackcurrant squash (undiluted)
- popping candy
- plastic cups
- straws
- teaspoons
- ice cream scoops

## The experience

<u>SAY:</u> **One way we celebrate Valentine's Day is by telling the special people in our lives how much we love them. Turn to a partner and tell them about someone you love. What's your favourite way to show that person you love him or her?**

Allow time for the discussions, and then invite a few children to share with the entire group.

Ask the children to wash their hands, then give each child a plastic cup. Help them fill the cups about one-third full with sparkling water. Then get them to add a small amount of blackcurrant squash. Next they can add one scoop of ice cream. Pause and let the children observe what happens. (They may need to push the ice cream down into the water with a teaspoon to get the full effect.)

<u>SAY:</u> **When we add the ice cream to the sparkling water, carbon dioxide moves out of the water and clusters around the air bubbles in the ice cream. This causes the air bubbles to expand, creating the fizzy, foamy drink.**

<u>ASK:</u> **How are the growing bubbles like God's love?**

<u>SAY:</u> **Let's see what the Bible says about loving others.**

Read 1 Thessalonians 3:12.

<u>SAY:</u> **God loves us so much that his love can overflow out of our lives, helping us love others.**

Ask the children to add more sparkling water to their cups.

<u>ASK:</u> **How is what happened to your water like this verse?**

**• Why do you think God's love for us makes our love for others grow and grow?**

**• What are ways others can *see* God's love through you?**

Get the children to sprinkle popping candy on top of their drinks and listen.

<u>ASK:</u> **What are ways others can *hear* God's love through you?**

Give straws to the children and let them enjoy their drinks.

# Unexpected valentine

BEST For All Ages

*After a rough day at school, Lucy finds a surprise valentine in a postbox.*

### SCRIPTURE

Genesis 1:1

### PROPS

- red postbox (a toy one or just a red box)
- letter in an envelope
- chair

### CAST

- Mum
- Lucy
- male narrator

### BEHIND THE SCENES

The simple set-up is just a chair at the right of the stage, with a red postbox or box placed beside it. Place the letter that Lucy will take out and read later in the sketch inside the box. The letter can be decorated however you wish.

## *Action!*

➡ *The scene begins with no actors onstage. The narrator speaks from offstage and addresses everyone in the room.*

### NARRATOR

Has anyone ever had a rough day? *(Pauses)* **Turn to the person next to you and tell them about a rough day you had recently.**

➡ *Allow about two minutes, and then continue.*

### NARRATOR

When you have a rough day, it can feel as if no one loves you. After your rough day, you may have felt something like this...

➡ *Mum is standing on the opposite side of the stage from the chair. Lucy walks in, and she's miserable. She had a rough day at school.*

### MUM

Hi, darling! How was school? Wasn't today your Valentine's Day party?

### LUCY

*(Shrugging)* Today Jenny told me the only reason anyone gave me any valentines was because they *had* to.

### MUM

Well, that wasn't a very nice thing to say.

### LUCY

But she's right. No one wants to give me anything because no one likes anything about me.

### MUM

Oh, darling, that's not true. You're amazing.

### LUCY

You have to say that. You're my mum.

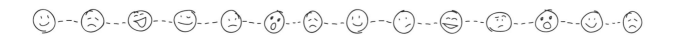

## MUM

Lucy, I'm sorry you feel that way. Let me finish dinner, and we'll talk about this more.

➡ *Mum exits and Lucy walks over and slumps in the chair. She looks down and notices the postbox and frowns, as if she's trying to work out what it's doing there.*

## LUCY

Mum! What's a postbox doing here?

➡ *There's no answer. Lucy shrugs and then opens the postbox. Inside, she finds a letter. She sits in the chair, a confused look still on her face. She opens the letter and, as she reads, we hear a voice.*

## NARRATOR

Dear Lucy, Happy Valentine's Day. This is a day to celebrate love—and you are very loved.

➡ *Lucy scoffs.*

## NARRATOR

What's the matter? Don't you believe me?

➡ *Lucy looks around, shocked that the voice seems to respond to her.*

## NARRATOR

You *are* loved. Not just by your parents and friends—but especially by me.
I knew you before you were born. I marvellously made you; I watched you being formed—and you're growing up wonderfully.

## LUCY

Huh?

## NARRATOR

I was so proud of you the other day when that little boy at the playground wanted a go on the swings and you got up and gave him your swing. *(Lucy looks surprised, as if to say, 'You saw me there?')* **And yesterday, when your mum had had such a bad day, you jumped in to help with dinner and then unloaded the dishwasher and finished your homework—all without complaining.** *(Lucy looks down at her feet, smiling, a bit embarrassed)* **That made me smile. Those pictures you draw—the ones your mum hangs on the fridge?** *(Lucy looks up)* **Those are beautiful, and I love how happy you are when you're painting.**

## LUCY

They *do* make me happy.

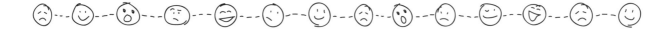

## NARRATOR

It's one of your gifts, and when you use it, it makes me very happy. I love so many things about you, and not just on Valentine's Day, but every day, because I made you to be very special. No matter what anyone else says.

## LUCY

Are you sure you know who you're talking to?

## NARRATOR

Lucy Jenkins. Age 10. Blonde hair, big blue eyes. Crooked teeth. Loves to sing and dance and paint beautiful pictures. Sometimes worries no one likes her, sometimes forgets to show others her sweet side. Talks to me at night before she goes to bed. Oh, I know who I'm talking about. Lucy Jenkins—you are loved.

## LUCY

Thanks, God. Happy Valentine's Day.

➡ *Lucy exits.*

## NARRATOR

And it's not just Lucy who's loved. It's everyone in this room. No matter how rough your day is, no matter how you feel, know that I love you. And you're the best valentine I could ever have!

BEST
Preschool
FOR

# God, how I love you

*Children sing about God's big, wide, deep love to the tune of 'Pop goes the weasel'.*

**SCRIPTURE**

Psalm 36

## Sing it!

**Your love is like a mountain,**

(make a mountain shape with both arms)

**Your love is like the ocean,**

(make wave motions with hands)

**Your love is big and wide and deep,**

(motion with hands for each: big, wide and deep)

**God, how I love you!**

(place hands over heart)

**All throughout the world,**

(sweep hands from left to right)

**And all throughout the Bible,**

(open hands like a book)

**Your love is big and wide and deep,**

(motion with hands for each: big, wide and deep)

**God, how I love you!**

(place hands over heart)

Extra-special FACTS

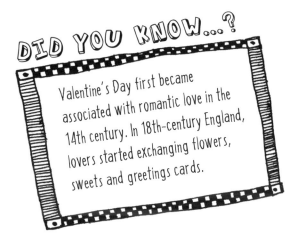

**DID YOU KNOW…?**

Valentine's Day first became associated with romantic love in the 14th century. In 18th-century England, lovers started exchanging flowers, sweets and greetings cards.

**DID YOU KNOW…?**

Legend has it that St Valentine, the martyred saint from ancient Rome after whom Valentine's Day is named, was killed for secretly marrying couples in defiance of an order of the Roman emperor. The emperor had forbidden marriage after Roman men began refusing to enlist, preferring to stay at home with their wives.

# True love

BEST
Primary Age
FOR

*Bring some Valentine's Day cheer to those who've lived— and loved—the longest.*

**SCRIPTURE**

James 1:27

**WHAT YOU'LL NEED**

- Bible
- card
- felt-tip pens
- stickers
- carnations or similar flowers

## The experience

Find a retirement home in your community and arrange with the manager a time around Valentine's Day when the children in your group can visit to chat with the residents and sing a song.

Meet with the children beforehand to prepare.

<u>SAY:</u> **Valentine's Day celebrates love and romance, but it can be a difficult day for those who are single, especially those people who have lost a husband or wife.**

Read aloud James 1:27.

Give the children card, felt-tip pens and stickers to make cards for the residents of the retirement home. Then learn and practise a song about God's love that you can sing to your valentine recipients.

Ask your church or the children (if appropriate) if they will donate some money to buy carnations; then deliver a flower and card to each resident of the retirement home on or around Valentine's Day. Serenade them with the song you have learnt. Encourage the children to show love by talking with the residents, using the questions below as a guide.

- What have you learned about love in your lifetime?
- How do you like to show people love?
- In what ways have people shown you love?
- What do you think of when you hear the word *love*?

JUST FOR FUN...

Attending a wedding for the first time, a little girl whispered to her mother, 'Why is the bride dressed in white?'

'Because white is the colour of happiness, and today is the happiest day of her life.'

The child thought about this for a moment, then said, 'So why is the groom wearing black?'

# Palm Sunday

Hosanna Hosanna

Less than a week before the crowds clamoured for Jesus' crucifixion, they hailed him as their king. Jesus, the humble king, rode through the streets of Jerusalem on a donkey, just as prophecies had foretold. The crowds spread their coats and palm branches on the road before Jesus and shouted his praises. Their excitement was growing so much that Matthew described the scene as an 'uproar' (New Living Translation). As children learn about this remarkable event, they'll discover how Jesus is worthy of their praise.

# True worship

*Children offer worship to the greatest celebrity of all.*

**SCRIPTURE**

Mark 11:1–11

**WHAT YOU'LL NEED**

- Bible
- green paper
- coloured paper

## The experience

Open your Bible at Mark 11:1–11.

SAY: **On Palm Sunday we remember when Jesus rode into Jerusalem on a donkey. The Bible says that huge crowds were excited and waiting for him as he entered the city.**

ASK: **When have you been part of a huge crowd? What was it like?**

SAY: **Let's see what it might have been like to be part of the crowd that followed Jesus on Palm Sunday.**

Form two groups. In one group, give each child a green sheet of paper to represent the palm branches. Give each child in the other group a coloured sheet of paper to represent the coats. Then ask the children to spread out around the room. Stand in the centre of the room.

Read Mark 11:8.

SAY: **The people in the crowd laid palm branches and coats on the road as Jesus rode through the city. They did this to praise him and show him respect.**

Ask the children to wave their green paper in the air, then put the coloured paper and green paper on the ground as they move towards the centre of the room, surrounding you.

Read Mark 11:9–10.

SAY: **The crowd surrounded Jesus. Then they shouted, 'Praise God! Blessings on the one who comes in the name of the Lord!' Let's shout, too!** Get the children to shout, 'Praise God! Blessings on the one who comes in the name of the Lord!' Then ask them to sit down.

ASK: **Tell us about a celebrity you'd be really excited to meet.**

- **How does the way you'd treat that celebrity compare to the way you treat Jesus each day?**

SAY: **People tend to worship celebrities, whether they're pop singers, actors or footballers. But Jesus is the only one worthy of our worship, and we can worship him every day. We can worship Jesus by singing, praying or serving him. Let's worship Jesus together with a praise prayer right now.**

Get the children to form a circle. Ask each child to name something he or she loves or knows about Jesus and then give the person to the right a high five. Continue around the circle until everyone has shared. Then pray: **Dear Jesus, we love you and praise you. Thank you for** [name some of the things the children have said]. **Amen.**

End by having a big round of applause for Jesus.

# Craft

# Donkey glove

BEST for Juniors

*Jesus asked for a donkey—so the children will make him one!*

## SCRIPTURE

Matthew 21:1–3

## WHAT YOU'LL NEED

- Bible
- 1 knitted glove per child
- polyester toy filling or cotton wool
- black wool
- black felt
- scissors
- small black beads or buttons
- hot-glue gun (adult use only)

## The experience

Read Matthew 21:1–3.

<u>SAY:</u> **Jesus needs a donkey—let's make some for him.**

**1.** Give each child one glove and enough filling to stuff its fingers and palm.

**2.** Ask them to turn the glove's cuff to the inside and tuck the thumb in approximately 2.5 cm, so the donkey's muzzle is shorter than its legs.

**3.** Cut eight 5 cm lengths of wool for the mane and three 8 cm lengths of wool for the tail. Children can work together to plait the tail and tie a knot on each end of the plait.

**4.** Fold the short wool pieces in half and glue them in the folded cuff of the glove over the thumb.

**5.** Glue one end of the tail in the folded cuff of the glove opposite the thumb. Fray the wool ends on the mane and the end of the tail.

**6.** Cut ear shapes from black felt. Glue each ear about 2 cm below the mane on either side of the glove, directly above the first finger.

**7.** Glue small black beads as eyes on either side of the glove.

**8.** Help the children to loop a 25 cm piece of wool around the donkey's muzzle, tying it under the muzzle. Then help them to run the long ends up over the donkey's back and tie them to form a bridle. Cut off excess wool.

# The wave parade

*With a ball and a passage from Mark, children will have fun trying to keep up with this fast-moving game.*

**SCRIPTURE**

Mark 11:8–10

**WHAT YOU'LL NEED**

- Bible
- ball

Extra-special
FACT

## DID YOU KNOW...?

There are over 2500 species of palm trees! In ancient Greek times, the leaves were used as a reward for the early Olympic games. They were also used by early Christians to celebrate victory, and were laid on the ground as Jesus entered Jerusalem—hence the name 'Palm Sunday'.

## The experience

Read aloud the account of Palm Sunday from Mark 11:8–10.

ASK: **Tell us about a time you were at a parade.**

SAY: **Sometimes you have to move to get a good view of what's happening at a parade. I imagine that's what happened to all the children who were there when Jesus entered town on Palm Sunday. Let's see how quick you are at moving your feet when something moves by.**

Form a line so the children are side by side, with about a metre between each person. (If you have more than ten children, form two groups.) Explain that you'll roll a ball down the line—and the ball will represent Jesus passing by.

SAY: **As soon as 'Jesus' passes you, you'll run to the far end of the line and stand next to the last person in line—that way you're ready to see the ball (I mean, Jesus) going by again. Our entire line will move, one person at a time. Got it? Let's start with a practice round.**

Roll the ball *very* slowly, so the children get the hang of running to the end of the line and taking a new place as the ball passes them. Try a few more times, rolling the ball more quickly each time. The children will most likely end up in a jumble, trying to get in line, but that's the point! Play several times, varying the speed of your roll.

SAY: **Palm Sunday was a big, noisy celebration—just like this was. Let's close with a celebration wave as Jesus passes by.** Roll the ball down the line, this time asking the children to cheer and wave as the ball goes by.

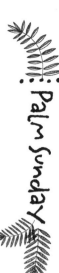
 Snack

BEST
All Ages
FOR

# Palm Sunday salad

*With lettuce 'palm branches' and a cucumber 'road', children will enjoy a healthy snack to celebrate Palm Sunday.*

## SCRIPTURE

Matthew 21:5

ALLERGY ALERT *see p. 7*

## WHAT YOU'LL NEED

- Bible
- paper plates
- baby carrots, cut in half
- cherry tomatoes, cut in half
- cucumbers, cut into thin strips
- lettuce leaves
- cheese slices
- forks

## The experience

Ask the children to wash their hands, then hand out the paper plates.

SAY: **The very first Palm Sunday was a very exciting day. Imagine for a moment what it would be like to be in town when, all of a sudden, Jesus comes riding along the road.** Ask the children to make a 'road' of cucumber strips down the centre of their plates. **A crowd had gathered—a big crowd full of people excited to see Jesus. Let's use our carrots and tomatoes**

to create a crowd in our town. Let the children line up their tomatoes and baby carrots on either side of the cucumber road. (They should be able to stand the carrots on the flat end where they were cut.)

SAY: **The crowd waved their palm leaves to welcome Jesus into the city. As he arrived, they threw their leaves on to the road to create a path for him and to worship him.** Ask the children to place lettuce 'palm leaves' along the cucumber road. **They also threw down their coats to help make the path for Jesus.** Place torn-up cheese slices along the cucumber road. **The crowd celebrated all day, and now we can celebrate with our very own Palm Sunday salad!**

Distribute forks, and ask the children to eat their salad as you discuss these questions.

ASK: **Why do you think the crowd was so excited to see Jesus?**

• **People in the crowd gave up their valuable coats in honour of Jesus. What would you give up in honour of him?**

Read Matthew 21:5.

SAY: **When Jesus came through town, the people recognised him as king—and they treated him like one. When we worship Jesus and make sacrifices for him, we're treating him like our king, too.**

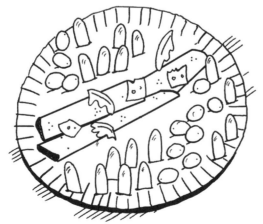

# It's a great day to sell palm leaves

The life of a palm-leaf salesman changes dramatically when demand for palm leaves increases on a particular day.

## SCRIPTURE

Matthew 21:1–11

## PROPS

- sign that reads, 'Palm leaves for sale, 3 for £1'
- table
- basket or box of palm leaves (these can be sugar paper cut-outs, made to look like palm leaves)

## CAST

- Marge
- Fred
- Man
- Woman
- Little boy

## BEHIND THE SCENES

The simple set-up is a table with the sign taped to it. Fred is holding the basket or box of palm leaves as his wife Marge walks in.

## Action!

**MARGE**

Fred, we need to talk.

**FRED**

Uh-oh.

**MARGE**

I've been a good wife. A great wife, some might say. When you wanted to go into this business, I stuck up for you and said you were creative. Said you were unique. But Fred? Something's got to give.

**FRED**

I know. It's been two years since I started selling the palm leaves. But I've got a good feeling!

**MARGE**

Two years, three months, 16 days to be exact. And how many leaves have you sold?

**FRED**

Well, just the one, but it was quite an important sale. I'm sure word is going to spread.

➡️ *Marge gives him a look that says she disagrees.*

**FRED**

I've got a feeling about today, Marge. I just have. God wouldn't have told me to do this for no reason.

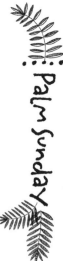

**MARGE**

I don't know... Let me know how it goes today.

➡ *Exits stage.*

*Fred crosses the stage to where his stall is set up and starts calling out to the people passing by.*

**FRED**

Palm leaves! Get your palm leaves here! Palm leaves, just three for a pound!

**MAN**

What a great idea! We can wave the palm leaves! You're a genius! I'll take three.

**FRED**

You will?

**MAN**

Of course! Great timing, man.

➡ *Fred is confused, but goes back to selling.*

**FRED**

Palm leaves! Get your palm leaves here! Palm leaves, just three for a pound.

**WOMAN**

These are just what we need! Perfect! I'll take one for each of my twelve children. We can wave them when he comes by. These are the perfect way to welcome him!

**FRED**

Welcome who?

**WOMAN**

You're funny. Thanks for the leaves! You're a genius!

**FRED**

Palm leaves! Get your palm leaves here! Palm leaves, just three for a pound!

**LITTLE BOY**

I don't have much money. *(Holds out a coin)* Will this buy me a leaf?

**FRED**

*(Takes the coin, and studies the little boy)* Of course. Why is buying a palm leaf so important to you?

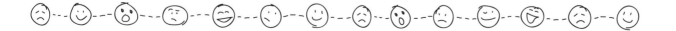

## LITTLE BOY

It's Jesus. He's coming here. Today. We're going to wave the leaves and welcome him like a king. Because that's what he is. He's coming now! I have to go!

➡ *Fred looks out across the audience at an imaginary Jesus riding by. He starts on the left and pans to the right, and near the end he stops, surprised.*

## FRED

He looked right at me. And he smiled. The King of kings.

## MAN

*(Running up)* We need more palm leaves! Hurry! We'll take all you have!

## FRED

He looked right at me...

➡ *Marge re-enters.*

## FRED

Marge! Look! I told you I had a feeling! Ha, ha!

## MARGE

Fred, I... I can't believe it!

➡ *Hugs Fred while jumping up and down.*

# Jesus came to town

*Celebrate with an easy-to-remember song that reminds little ones of when Jesus came to Jerusalem. Sing to the tune of 'London Bridge is falling down'.*

**SCRIPTURE**

Matthew 21:1–11

## Sing it!

**Jesus came to town one day,**
*(move your right arm as if to say 'Come here')*

**Town one day, town one day,**
*(move your left arm in the same way, then your right arm again)*

**Jesus came to town one day,**
*(move your right arm as if to say 'Come here')*

**He waved as he went by.**
*(wave right hand)*

**People waved their palms that day,**
*(wave right hand)*

**Palms that day, palms that day,**
*(wave left hand, then right hand)*

**People waved their palms that day,**
*(wave right hand)*

**They waved as he went by.**
*(wave both hands)*

### Extra-special FACTS

**DID YOU KNOW...?**

Certain types of palm trees grow fruit. Among them, the Guadalupe Palm, the Chilean Wine Palm and the Jelly Palm, which is native to Brazil and used for, you've guessed it, jellies and jams.

**DID YOU KNOW...?**

On Palm Sunday, some churches hand out small biscuits with an image of a lamb to congregation members. These are called pax cakes. ('Pax' is Latin for 'peace'.)

BEST Primary Age FOR

# Victory palm branches

*Children make posters to encourage hospital patients.*

**SCRIPTURE**

Romans 8:35–37

**WHAT YOU'LL NEED**

- Bible
- A5 card
- art supplies such as felt-tip pens, crayons, colouring pencils and glitter glue
- green sugar paper
- scissors
- glue
- clear self-adhesive covering film

Can anything ever separate us from Christ's love? Does it mean he no longer loves us if we have trouble or calamity, or are persecuted, or hungry, or destitute, or in danger, or threatened with death? ... No, despite all these things, overwhelming victory is ours through Christ, who loved us.
ROMANS 8:35, 37

## The experience

Contact a local hospital or hospice and ask for permission to put posters in a waiting area or ward where patients can take one if they wish. Once you have permission, get your children together to create the posters.

<u>SAY:</u> **In Roman times, palm branches were symbols of triumph and winning, both in games and military campaigns. When Jesus rode into Jerusalem, the Jewish people honoured him by lining the road with palm branches because they expected him to bring victory over the Roman rulers. Today when we think of winning, we don't usually think of palm leaves.**

<u>ASK:</u> **What things symbolise winning today?**

Ask the children to cut palm leaves from sugar paper and stick them on to posters on which the following words from Romans 8 are displayed:

*Can anything ever separate us from Christ's love? Does it mean he no longer loves us if we have trouble or calamity, or are persecuted, or hungry, or destitute, or in danger, or threatened with death? ... No, despite all these things, overwhelming victory is ours through Christ, who loved us.*
ROMANS 8:35, 37

They can also decorate the posters using felt-tip pens, crayons, coloured pencils or glitter glue. When the posters are complete, laminate them with self-adhesive covering film.

Read Romans 8:35–37.

<u>SAY:</u> **There are people in our community who are threatened with death or injury, and they might feel like they're separated from Jesus' love.**

Ask the children to hold up their posters and take turns praying for strength and courage for the people who will see them. Then take them to the hospital or hospice. Alternatively, the children can take their posters home to give to someone they know.

# REBIRTH EASTER

**Bible Focus**

**Washed away**
*page 42*

**Craft**

**Stones cry out**
*page 43*

**Sliding stone**
*page 44*

**Game**

**A common thread**
*page 46*

**Snack**

**Good news bouquet**
*page 47*

**Stained-glass cross cookies**
*page 48*

**Sketch**

**The box of stones**
*page 49*

**Song**

**I'm the life, the truth, the way**
*page 53*

**Outreach**

**Food to spare**
*page 54*

Darkness consumed the earth. Earthquakes shattered rocks. Women wept. And then, after Jesus' friends placed him in the tomb, there was silence. On the third day, though, there was confusion followed by glorious rejoicing as Jesus' followers found his empty tomb and learnt that he'd come back to life. When children celebrate Jesus' resurrection, they see that thanks to his victory over death we can have new life in Jesus.

# Washed away

*Children see how their sins can vanish as Jesus conquers death!*

**SCRIPTURE**

1 Corinthians 15:54–57

**WHAT YOU'LL NEED**

- Bible
- baby wipes
- washable felt-tip pens
- cups
- lukewarm water
- washing-up liquid
- plastic bags

## The experience

Give each child a baby wipe, and ask them to write or draw several things they've done wrong on the wipes. Younger children can just make marks on the wipes to represent wrong things.

SAY: **Jesus died on the cross to forgive us for our sins—for everything we've ever done wrong. His friends and family thought the story ended there with his death. Write the word** *death* **on top of all your sins.** Younger children can just scribble all over their marks.

Give each child a cup with a small amount of washing-up liquid and some lukewarm water. Make sure they place the cup on top of a plastic bag to catch any drips. Then ask them to place their wipes into the cups and swirl them around as you read 1 Corinthians 15:54–57.

SAY: **But Jesus' story didn't end with sin and death. He won! Lift your wipes out of the water and see what has happened to your sin.** Allow time for the children to see that their wipes are now completely clean.

ASK: **How does this experience remind you of Jesus' forgiveness?**

• **What's one thing you can tell others that Easter means to you?**

SAY: **At Easter, we know that Jesus died for our sins so we can be forgiven. And we celebrate Jesus defeating death because we know he took away our sins once and for all. And best of all, he wants us to live with him in heaven forever.**

△ ▽ △ ▽ △ ▽ △ ▽ **Craft** ▽ △ ▽ △ ▽ △ ▽ △ ▽

# Stones cry out

*Children create keepsake rocks to remind them of what Jesus did for us.*

### SCRIPTURE

Luke 19:39–40; Luke 22:39–41; Matthew 27:50–51; Luke 23:53; Luke 24:2–3

### WHAT YOU'LL NEED

- Bible
- stones of various shapes, 5 per child
- fine-tipped permanent markers
- paper bags or small gift boxes
- stickers and felt-tip pens

## The experience

Ask the children to talk about interesting rocks or rock formations they've seen.

SAY: **Stones and rocks are mentioned more than 400 times in the Bible. People used them to build altars to remember what God had done. Jesus told stories about stones. Stones were part of the landscape at the end of Jesus' life, too. Today we're going to make a rock collection to help us remember the story of Jesus' death and resurrection.**

Give each child five stones and a permanent marker. SAY: **On the Sunday before he died, Jesus rode into Jerusalem. The people waved palm branches and praised him. And Jesus said something about rocks. Let's see what he said.** Read Luke 19:39–40. Ask the children to draw a palm branch on a stone to represent the crowd's praise.

ASK: **What are some of the ways you praise Jesus?**

SAY: **On the night before he died, Jesus prayed in the garden of Gethsemane. The Bible uses a stone as a measurement of where Jesus went to pray.** Read Luke 22:39–41. Invite the children to draw a flower to represent the garden on one of the stones.

ASK: **What do you need to pray about?** (Let the children answer silently or to the group.)

SAY: **When Jesus was on the cross, something happened to the rocks nearby.** Read Matthew 27:50–51. Ask the children to draw a lightning bolt on one rock to represent the stones splitting.

ASK: **How do you feel about such a powerful God?**

SAY: **After Jesus died, a man named Joseph took Jesus' body from the cross and laid it in a tomb.** Read Luke 23:53. Invite the children to draw a cross on one of the rocks.

ASK: **Talk about something that makes you sad.**

SAY: **The reason people realised Jesus was alive had to do with a rock.** Read Luke 24:2–3. Ask the children to draw an arrow on one of their stones to show that it rolled aside.

ASK: **Tell us about a time you celebrated something.**

SAY: **The events of Easter start out sad; but in the end we see God's power, and we have reason to celebrate! Whenever you look at your stone collection, remember to praise Jesus for his power over death. Now let's decorate a place where you can keep your stones.** Let the children use felt-tip pens and stickers to decorate their paper bags or gift boxes and then place their stones inside.

△ ▽ △ ▽ △ ▽ △ ▽ △ ▽ △ ▽ △ ▽ △ ▽ △ **43**

# Sliding stone

*BEST Primary Age FOR*

*Children see the stone roll away in this exciting diorama.*

### SCRIPTURE

Matthew 28:2–4

### WHAT YOU'LL NEED

- Bible
- small empty boxes (with lids)
- scissors
- black and grey card
- grey and white paint
- paintbrushes
- clear sticky tape
- black sugar paper
- wooden lollipop craft sticks
- fake grass or green sugar paper
- pebbles
- hot-glue gun (adult use only)
- yellow cellophane or tissue paper

## The experience

Read Matthew 28:2–4.

<u>SAY:</u> **It must have been quite a sight to see the stone rolled away and the tomb empty! Let's make a diorama—or a miniature scene— to see what it may have looked like.**

**1.** Help the children to cut a piece of black or grey card the width and height of the inside of the box. Then ask them to crumple and uncrumple the card. They can dab grey and

*Tip* Want to go all out? Use black foam board to create your tomb wall and stone. Add texture by hammering the foam board. In addition to the pebbles and grass, use sand and twigs to make the front of the tomb look authentic.

white paint on the crumpled card to make the surface look like a stone wall.

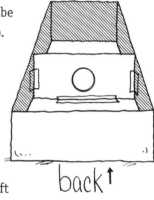

**2.** Cut out a circle approximately 6 cm in diameter from the bottom centre of the card, and set it aside. This shape will be the stone, and the hole will be the opening of the tomb.

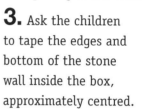

**3.** Ask the children to tape the edges and bottom of the stone wall inside the box, approximately centred.

back↑

**4.** Help them to tape one end of a wooden craft stick to the lower part of the back of the stone shape, then paint the front of the craft stick to match the stone.

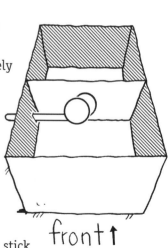

**5.** Just in front of the stone wall, help the children to cut a small vertical slit approximately 1.5 cm long in the side of the box, near the bottom. From the inside of the box, slip the empty end of the craft stick through the slit and then align the stone with the tomb opening. The craft stick should extend out of the side of the box.

front↑↑

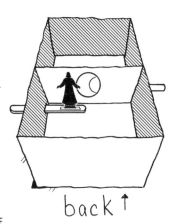

**6.** Using the pattern to the right, help each child cut a figure of Jesus out of black sugar paper. Then fold along the line and tape a craft stick to the bottom of the folded tab. Help the children cut a horizontal slit in the side of the box, close to the bottom of the box, about 2.5 cm behind the stone wall. Slide the stick through the slit from the inside so Jesus lines up with the tomb opening.

back ↑

**7.** Let the children use the fake grass and pebbles to create a scene in the front half of the box. Hot glue everything in place.

**8.** Help the children cut an 8 cm hole in the back of the box, behind the tomb opening. They can use sticky tape to cover the hole with yellow cellophane or tissue paper. In the front end of the box, help them cut a viewing hole approximately 4 cm in diameter. They can use tape to cover the lid of the box with yellow cellophane or tissue paper (front half) and black sugar paper (back half).

**9.** Get the children to stand under a light and tell the Easter story as they re-enact it with their dioramas. They should start with both craft sticks pulled all the way to the edge. As they talk about how Jesus was buried in the tomb, they can slide him forwards so he can be seen. Then they can slide the stone to cover the tomb entrance. When they tell about Easter morning, get them to slide Jesus to the side and then pull back the stone to reveal the empty, shining tomb!

back          front

# A common thread

BEST
Primary Age
FOR

*Children discover a common thread that shows we're all connected to Jesus' sacrifice.*

### SCRIPTURE

Mark 16:1–7

### WHAT YOU'LL NEED

- Bible
- ball of wool
- small wooden cross

Extra-special
**FACT**

**DID YOU KNOW…?**

UK sales of Cadbury's Creme Eggs peaked in 2006. Creme Eggs are still leading as the most popular Easter egg against mini eggs, but the gap is narrowing!

## The experience

Ask the children to form a big circle. Keeping the cross hidden from view, hold up the ball of wool and <u>SAY</u>: **Let's see how tangled up we can get! We have 60 seconds. I'll hold on to this end of the wool, and I'll throw the ball to someone else in the circle. Once you get it, hang on to the wool at the point you caught it, and throw the ball to someone else. The only rule is that you can't hand the ball of wool to the person next to you. One minute. Ready? Go!**

While the children are busy throwing the wool, tie your end of the wool to the cross. When time is up, turn to the person holding the ball and <u>SAY</u>:

- **Talk about a time when someone did something amazing for you that made you feel really special.**

After that child has shared, ask him or her to bring the ball, untangling as necessary, back to the next person holding the strand. That person will wind the excess wool back on to the ball. Continue with the same question for each person (even when children go twice), until the ball is back to you.

Hold up the cross that's now attached to the wool and <u>SAY</u>: **Through all of us there is a common thread. Just as you shared about people in your lives doing amazing things for you, Jesus did something amazing for all of us 2000 years ago on a cross. And a most amazing thing happened two days later.**

Read Mark 16:1–7.

<u>ASK</u>: **What amazes you about Jesus?**

- **Turn to the person next to you and find a 'common thread' between you.**

<u>SAY</u>: **Jesus gave his life for each of you. It's the one thing that ties us back to him, and when we tell others about how amazing Jesus is, it's like throwing a ball of wool to them. It connects you, just as you're connected to Jesus!**

# Good news bouquet

*As children create these edible bouquets, they'll learn that they're alive with Jesus!*

## SCRIPTURE

Romans 6:7–10

## WHAT YOU'LL NEED

- Bible
- clear plastic cups
- bitesize Shredded Wheat® or similar
- marshmallows
- kebab skewers
- bowls
- white icing
- plastic knives
- sprinkles or other cake decorations
- green sugar paper
- scissors
- sticky tape

## The experience

SAY: **Easter is a time when we remember life. Trees sprout leaves; animals that were hibernating come out; and, most importantly, Jesus came back to life!**

ASK: **Name things that are alive. How do you know those things are alive?**

SAY: **One thing that dies every winter but comes back to life in the spring is a flower. Let's make some edible flowers.** Set out the ingredients. Place the icing and sprinkles in bowls.

Get the children to wash their hands, then fill the clear plastic cups with Shredded Wheat®. Then help them to stick a marshmallow on a kebab skewer (watch that younger children don't pierce themselves—or others!). The

children can use a plastic knife to spread icing on the marshmallow, then they can roll the iced marshmallow in the sprinkles, creating the flower and stem. Ask the children to place the flower in the cup and make two more like it.

Give out green sugar paper and help the children to cut out leaves and tape them to the skewer stems. For younger children, simply tear small scraps of green paper and help them tape them on to the stems.

Let the children enjoy their snack as you read Romans 6:7–10.

SAY: **Our flowers can remind us that Jesus died on the cross for our sins and came back to life. Because Jesus came back to life, we can have a new life, too.**

ASK: **How can you tell if someone is alive in Jesus?**

SAY: **Think about some of the bad things in your life that seem to have power over you. For example, maybe it's hard for you not to be mean to your brother. Or maybe you use naughty words. Say a silent prayer that Jesus will help you see how he can help you with all those things.**

Allow a few moments and then PRAY: **Dear God, thank you for taking away our sins, not just so you could forgive us, but also so you could help us do the right thing. In Jesus' name, Amen**

# Stained-glass cross cookies

*Children journey to the cross with this sweet treat.*

## SCRIPTURE

Acts 13:29–31

## WHAT YOU'LL NEED

- Bible
- red boiled sweets
- sandwich bags
- rolling pins
- baking trays
- baking paper
- cookie dough, chilled
- flour
- tablespoon
- cross-shaped cookie cutters in varying sizes (available online)
- butter knives
- cooling racks
- spatula
- oven (adult use only)
- oven glove
- paper plates

## The experience

Get the children to wash their hands.

SAY: **The cross is a very important symbol for us. Jesus died on the cross, stained with his blood, so our sins could be forgiven. Let's roll out our cookie dough and cut crosses to remind us of what Jesus did for us. As you cut your cross, think about things you've done wrong. Those are the things Jesus died to forgive.**

Preheat an oven to 180°C (160°C fan, gas mark 4). Coat the cookie dough with two tablespoons of flour. Roll out the dough on a clean, flat surface, using additional flour as needed to prevent sticking. Get the children to cut out the dough with floured, large cross-shaped cookie cutters. With smaller cross cookie cutters or butter knives, help the children to cut out the centre of the cookie, leaving a frame of about 1.5 cm. Line baking trays with baking paper and place the cookies on it.

SAY: **Let's hammer some red sweets to remind us how Jesus was nailed to the cross. As you crush your sweets, ask Jesus to forgive you for the things you've done wrong.**

Give each child three or four red boiled sweets, and help them to crush the sweets in a sandwich bag with a rolling pin.

SAY: **Let's put our crushed sweets into the crosses to remind us of Jesus' blood. As you put your sweets into your cross, thank Jesus for what he did for you.**

Help the children to fill the cookie cut-outs with the crushed sweets, making sure the sweets touch the edge of the cookie. Avoid mounding the crushed sweets in tall heaps.

SAY: **Now we'll put our cookies in the oven to remind us that Jesus went into a tomb. Smell the sweetness of the baking cookies and praise Jesus for his sweet love for you.**

Bake the cookies until the edges are light golden brown and the crushed sweets have melted. Cool for a few minutes on the baking trays until the crushed sweets have hardened. Place the cookies on cooling racks and cool for about 15 minutes. Read Acts 13:29–31.

SAY: **Even though Jesus died on the cross and was buried in a tomb, he came back to life. That's what we celebrate at Easter! Let's eat our cookies to remind us that the tomb is empty and our sins are gone!**

Enjoy the cookies with your children as you discuss these questions.

ASK: **What were some things you talked to Jesus about as you made these cookies?**

- **What will you do this week to celebrate that Jesus lives?**

# The box of stones

BEST Juniors FOR

*A poignant sketch that will help turn children's hearts towards Jesus.*

### SCRIPTURE

Romans 6:8–9

### PROPS

- cardboard box filled with stones for each character.
- 10 small stones, labelled: 'disobedience to parents', 'swearing', 'cheating on a maths test', 'shoplifting', 'cheating', 'making fun of people', 'telling a big lie', 'hatred', 'complaining' and 'lying'
- card table
- 2 chairs
- large cross
- small stone for each audience member
- Joe Strock's *Surrender* album (available as CD, on iTunes, Google Play and Spotify)
- 'Come to Jesus' from Chris Rice's *Run the Earth, Watch the Sky* albums (available as CD, on iTunes, Google Play and Spotify)
- CD player or other means to play the music

### CAST

- Main character (a child)
- Three child 'friends', two male and one female
- Therapist (adult female, wearing a suit)
- Jesus (wearing a white robe and a crown of thorns)
- Adult dressed in dark clothing
- Narrator (adult)

### BEHIND THE SCENES

The therapist's office is set up with the table and chairs on the left-hand side of the stage. The large cross is set up on the opposite side.

Give a small stone to each person in the audience.

## Action!

➡ *The main character enters from stage right, slowly moving towards centre stage during the first paragraph. He or she struggles with a heavy load—a large cardboard box filled with stones.*

### MAIN CHARACTER

**I'm not exactly sure where it came from, this box of stones. It seems like I've been carrying it around all my life. It didn't used to be this heavy. It's sort of strange, but the older I get, the heavier it becomes.** *(Looks tired; droops shoulders)* **And as each day goes by, more and more stones get in my box.** *(Sets box on the floor and sits beside it)*
**I can barely remember finding the first stone. I think I was around four years old. I lied to my parents about breaking a vase. It was no big deal—but after I lied, that's when I noticed this box with a single stone inside. I pulled out the stone...**

➡ *The main character reaches into the box and searches through different stones, not finding the right one at first. He finds it and continues.*

### MAIN CHARACTER

**Yeah, here it is. The first stone. I pulled it out of the box... It was filthy.** *(Wipes*

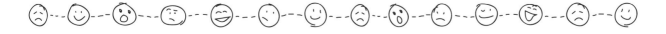

*stone on clothes)* **It had the word 'lying' on it. I just threw it back in the box.** *(Puts it back in the box)* **No big deal. After all, it was just a little lie.**

➡ *The main character pauses for a brief second, then shakes his head.*

## MAIN CHARACTER

**Yeah, right. It was no big deal—so why did I feel so bad? Why did I feel that no one could ever love me?**

➡ *The main character pauses again, looking into the box.*

## MAIN CHARACTER

**But now I have so many of these stones.** *(Reaches in and pulls out a stone)* **This one: 'disobedience to parents'—so what? All they ever do is gripe at me anyway.** *(Puts the stone in the box and pulls out another)* **'Swearing'. It's really tough to stop a bad word slipping out every now and then.** *(Pulls stones out faster and reads them)* **Cheating on a maths test, shoplifting, cheating again, making fun of people, telling a big lie, hatred, complaining, lying again.**

➡ *The main character hangs his head in desperation. Then he puts the stones back in the box.*

## MAIN CHARACTER

**Before I knew it, I was carrying around this heavy box of stones.** *(Slowly struggles to lift the box again)* **Each stone is a reminder of bad things—the heaviness of sin in my life. I feel so bad. Why have I done these things? Could anyone ever love me enough to forgive me?**

➡ *The main character bows his head, and as he does, the track 'He is all you need' by Joe Strock begins to play.*

## MAIN CHARACTER

**I'm afraid to talk to my parents about all my stones. I know they'd really be disappointed in me. I tried talking to a friend about it.**

➡ *Friend #1 enters from stage right with his box.*

## MAIN CHARACTER

**He took a stone out of the box.** *(Friend #1 sets down his box and takes a stone from the main character's box. Friend #1 smiles as he looks at it)* **He said, 'What are you worried about? It's just a little sin!' Then he put the stone back in the box.** *(Friend #1 exits with his box stage left)*

➡ *Friend #2 enters from stage right with her box.*

## MAIN CHARACTER

**Another friend was so shocked by what she read on the stones that she put them back in the box, looked at me with disgust and walked away.** *(Friend #2 sets down her box, peeks into the main character's box, looks shocked, picks up her own box, walks away and exits stage left)*

➡ *Friend #3 enters from stage right with his box.*

## MAIN CHARACTER

**A close friend even helped me carry the box of stones around... but over time, it got too heavy and wore him down, too.** *(Friend #3 tries to carry the main character's box and his own box. He eventually stumbles and lets go. Looks apologetic as he exits stage left with his box)*

## MAIN CHARACTER

**It's OK; he had his own box of stones to carry. It was nice of him to help, but it was just too much weight to carry.**

➡ *The therapist enters from stage left and sets her box on the table. The main character carries his box and joins the therapist at the table.*

## MAIN CHARACTER

**Somebody told me I should see a therapist. That was OK for a while. I would go into her office and empty the** box of stones on to the table. *(Empties box of stones on to the table)* **We talked about the stones—and believe me, that wasn't easy.** *(Both look at the stones as though analysing them)* **After looking through my stones, she told me it wasn't my fault. I was a victim. It was everyone else's fault. It felt good to talk about it, but after every session I'd pack the stones back in my box and drag them home.**

➡ *The main character places his box on the floor and drags it to centre stage. The therapist exits stage left with her box.*

## MAIN CHARACTER

**I wish someone could help me. I'm so tired of stumbling under this load. I want some help! I want some relief! I want someone to love me and forgive me.** *(Bows head with shoulders drooped and hand to forehead)*

➡ *Song segment: play 'How could you say no?' by Joe Strock as Jesus enters from stage left and slowly walks to the main character. Jesus places his hand on the main character's shoulder, takes the box of stones, and slowly walks to the cross. Jesus empties the stones one by one at the foot of the cross, then takes his place on the cross. The main character and the person dressed in dark clothing take Jesus off the cross and slowly carry him as they exit stage right. The narrator enters from stage left.*

## NARRATOR

**Behold, the Lamb of God, who takes away the sin of the world. God made Jesus— who knew no sin—to become sin that we might be made right with God. Jesus was wounded for all our sins. He was bruised for all the things we've done wrong. And by his punishment, we are healed.**

➡ *This next segment is directed to the audience.*

## NARRATOR

**You've been holding a stone that represents sin in your life. In a moment, you'll have time to give it to Jesus and lay it at the foot of the cross. You'll take** **nothing away. Because of our Saviour's death on the cross and resurrection from the dead, you are free!**

➡ *As children lay their stones at the cross and return to their seats, play 'The cross' by Joe Strock. After the last person is seated, darken the room and then play 'Come to Jesus' by Chris Rice.*

*The main character slowly enters and kneels at the cross. On the third chorus, turn on the stage lights as Jesus enters in a white robe. Jesus walks over to the cross, places his hand on the main character's shoulder and whispers in his ear. The main character is startled as he stands up and steps back from Jesus. Jesus opens his arms. They embrace and exit arm in arm.*

# I'm the life, the truth, the way

**BEST** Preschool **FOR**

*Celebrate Easter with easy-to-learn lyrics, set to the tune of the 'A, B, C' song.*

**SCRIPTURE**

John 14:6

## Sing it!

**Jesus came to earth to say,**

*(touch a finger to each palm; then cup your hands around your mouth as if calling out)*

**'I'm the life, the truth, the way.'**

*(right thumb up, left thumb up, then raise both hands up)*

**Gave his life for you and me,**

*(point to others and then to yourself)*

**Gave his life to set us free.**

*(put your hands over your face; then open them on 'free')*

**Jesus came to earth to say,**

*(touch a finger to each palm; then cup your hands around your mouth as if calling out)*

**'I'm the life, the truth, the way.'**

*(right thumb up, left thumb up, then raise both hands up)*

CHURCH SIGNS SEEN AT EASTER

Jesus paid the price.
You get to keep the change.

Lent:
spring training for Christians
Easter:
OPENING DAY

BEST All Ages FOR

# Food to spare

*Jesus told Peter, 'Feed my lambs'—so children will do just that with some Easter treats.*

### SCRIPTURE

John 21:4–6, 12–13, 15–17

### WHAT YOU'LL NEED

- Bible
- small, clean plastic jars
- mini chocolate eggs and other Easter treats
- colourful card
- hole punch
- felt-tip pens
- ribbons

## The experience

In the weeks leading up to this project, collect small, clean jars and remove the labels.

Gather your children and <u>SAY</u>: **After Jesus came back to life, he appeared to his disciples. When he said 'Feed my lambs,' he meant more than just giving people food. He meant looking after them in any way they needed. But he also made sure his disciples had plenty of food to eat.**

<u>ASK</u>: **Talk about a time you were really hungry.**

Read John 21:4–6, 12–13.

<u>SAY</u>: **Then Jesus told Peter how to show that he really loved Jesus.** Read John 21:15–17.

<u>ASK</u>: **Tell us about a time you shared food with someone.**

<u>SAY</u>: **There are people in our town who are hungry. And we can show Jesus' love by feeding his lambs a special Easter treat!**

Get the children to fill the jars with mini eggs and other treats, and to write notes or poems on colourful card. Punch a hole in the corner of each card and string a piece of ribbon through the hole. Tie one note around each jar just underneath the lid. Give the goodies to a local food bank, or let the children take them home to give to neighbours as an Easter outreach.

*Tip* Want to go the extra mile? The week before this activity, ask the children to bring in donations of food for your local food bank. Check in advance with the food bank about what items they need.

# Mother's Day

I ♥ MUM

Mother's Day, or Mothering Sunday, isn't just a recent invention; celebrations honouring mothers have taken place for hundreds of years, including in the 17th century, when Christians in England dedicated a day to honouring Jesus' mother, Mary. That special day was later expanded to include all mothers. Today, cultures everywhere celebrate mums and special women who serve as mums. With these ideas, children can honour their mothers and special women in their lives as they recognise the blessings they give.

# The best mum

*Children think about
what their mothers do.*

**SCRIPTURE**

Proverbs 31:13–29

**WHAT YOU'LL NEED**

• Bibles
• paper
• pens

## The experience

Form small groups of children, with no more than 17 groups. Split the verses of Proverbs 31:13–29 among the groups as evenly as possible.

SAY: **The Bible has a lot to say about mums. You've each got Bible verses about awesome mums. A lot of this passage talks about what mums did back in Bible times. Maybe mums today don't do all those things any more—but they do similar things. Your job is to read your verses and see if you can spot anything that reminds you of** *your* **mum or someone who's like a mum to you. For example, verse 13 says, 'She finds wool and flax and busily spins it.' Maybe your mum does some sewing, or maybe she takes you to buy clothes.**

Allow time for the children to read and think about their verses. Then distribute paper and pens, and ask them to rewrite their verses to better describe today's mums.

ASK: **What did you notice about how mums' roles have changed or stayed the same?**

• **What do you most appreciate about what your mum does?**

When the children have finished, ask them to come up to the front of the room and stand in a line in order of their verses. Then go down the line, letting the children read the rewritten verses. Practise a few times. Then plan a time for mothers to come in to see the presentation, or see if you can get a few minutes during the main church service for the children to present their verses to the congregation.

*Tip If you're planning to let the children present their verses to the church, encourage them to bring in props that help demonstrate what they are saying.*

# Mum's a gem

BEST
Primary Age
FOR

*Mums are more precious than rubies—and this craft will remind children of this.*

## SCRIPTURE

Proverbs 31:10

## WHAT YOU'LL NEED

- laptop and colour printer
- internet access
- paper
- pens or pencils
- inexpensive A4 frames (available at bargain and craft stores)
- stick-on gems or Bendaroos™

## The experience

SAY: **Our mums are gems! Proverbs 31:10 says this about a good mum: 'She is more precious than rubies.' Rubies are very valuable red jewels or gems. Our mums are special and precious to us. Take a few minutes to think of words that describe your mum, a grandmother or aunt, or another woman in your life who takes care of you. To help you get started, think of words that could finish this sentence: 'My mum is...' Write those words.**

Hand out paper and pencils. Allow time for the children to complete the task.

SAY: **Now we're going to add your word list into a computer program that's going to make a super-cool word collage called a word cloud. You'll need at least twelve words to make your word cloud look good. The more words, the better it will turn out. Then we'll put it into a picture frame and you'll get to decorate the frame and give it to your mum on Mother's Day.**

When the children have their word lists, visit www.wordle.net and click 'Create your own'.

Type a child's words into the box labelled 'Paste in a bunch of text'. Click 'Go'. If the children want certain words to appear larger than others, type in those words multiple times. The more times you enter a word, the larger it will appear.

Let the children each choose a font, layout and colour scheme. Then print the word clouds.

Help the children put their unique word clouds into frames, then let them decorate the frames with stick-on gems or Bendaroos™.

Tip: If you don't have access to a laptop in your room, get the children to write their list in advance, then input their words at home. On Mother's Day, hand out the word clouds and let the children decorate their frames.

# Mum's coffee holder

**BEST Primary Age FOR**

*Children make keepsake coffee-cup holders for their mums.*

### SCRIPTURE

Proverbs 23:25

### WHAT YOU'LL NEED

- Bible
- cardboard coffee-cup sleeves (available online)
- different-coloured 23 cm x 30 cm craft foam sheets
- scissors
- felt-tip pens
- assorted foam stickers
- adhesive Velcro® strips

## The experience

Read aloud Proverbs 23:25.

SAY: **Raise your hand if your mum works hard.** Pause. **Mums have a lot to do, and one thing that many mums like is coffee—because it keeps them energised. So we're going to make coffee holders for our mums.**

**1.** Pull open the cardboard coffee sleeves, and use the cardboard as a template for children to trace on to the craft foam. Help the children cut out their sleeve shapes.

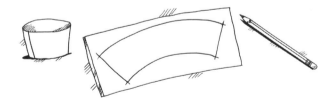

**2.** Ask the children to write a message on the coffee sleeves. For example, they could write 'Happy Mother's Day' or 'I love you, Mum' and decorate the foam sleeves with foam stickers.

**3.** Stick Velcro® strips on the ends of the sleeves, so the ends overlap by approximately 2 cm and stick together.

Encourage the children to take their coffee holders home to give to their mothers. (Mothers should perhaps be warned to check the quality of their child's workmanship before trusting their hot drinks to it!)

End by praying as a group for all the children's mothers. Pray that God will give mothers the energy they need.

*Mother's Day*

# She knows me so well

**BEST FOR** Primary Age

*This game reminds children just how much their mums love them.*

**SCRIPTURE**

Matthew 6:25–32

**WHAT YOU'LL NEED**

- Bible
- 5 items, each of a very different shape and weight; for example, a pair of balled-up socks, a tennis ball, a set of keys, a beach ball and a Frisbee

## The experience

SAY: **On Mother's Day, we celebrate mums. And if anyone deserves a celebration, it's mums. Some days we ask our mums, 'When will I eat?' or 'What can I do?' or 'What should I wear?' Listen to what the Bible says about what we need.** Read Matthew 6:25–32. **We're important to God—and we're important to our mums, too. Like God, our mums love us and know exactly what we need exactly when we need it. In fact, they might even know what we need before we ask.**

**Let's take a minute and think of all the things that mums give us or do for us when we need it.** Allow one minute for the children to call out ideas.

SAY: **I'm going to give you a chance to see how much mums love us.**

Form a circle and let each child say his or her name so others know it. Encourage the children to throw one of the items around the circle in a pattern, with each child saying the name of the person they're about to throw the item to. Let the children get comfortable with the pattern—it should feel easy. After a few times around, add one more item. Throw the second item right after the first in a rhythm. After a few tries, add in another item... then another... and another! If a child drops the item, he or she picks it up quickly and continues the pattern. After a few rounds, gather the items.

ASK: **What was easy or difficult about this game?**

• **How is this game like or unlike what mums do for us?**

• **How can we thank our mums for all they do to take care of us?**

SAY: **One thing that mums are never too busy for is a hug! So be sure to give yours a good, long, heartfelt hug today.**

# Soup for Mum

BEST
All Ages
FOR

*Children make this meal for later to save their mums the trouble of cooking on Mother's Day.*

**SCRIPTURE**

Exodus 20:12

**WHAT YOU'LL NEED**

- Bible
- self-adhesive address labels
- 500 g dried lentils
- 500 g split green peas
- 500 g pearl barley
- 500 g brown rice
- 500 g alphabet macaroni
- 2 cups of chopped onions
- large bowl
- stirring spoon
- cups for measuring
- resealable sandwich bags
- index cards
- felt-tip pens
- sticky tape

## The experience

Preprint the following instructions on address labels: 'Add 6 cups of water, and simmer for 1½ hours. Add fresh ingredients if desired, such as celery, shredded cabbage, tomatoes or leftover meat.'

SAY: **Today we're celebrating Mother's Day.**

Read aloud Exodus 20:12.

ASK: **What does it mean to honour your mother?**

SAY: **To honour someone means to respect them and to do everything you can to help them and please them.**

ASK: **What can you do to honour your mother?**

SAY: **One way we can honour our mums is to help with dinner. We're going to make something that will honour your mums by helping them.**

Ask the children to wash their hands, then get them to help you pour all of the food ingredients into a large bowl and stir them. Then let each child scoop 1½ cups of the mixture into a sandwich bag.

Give each child a preprinted label to stick to his or her bag.

Then give them an index card and ask them to write or draw how they'll help their mum to cook the meal, such as setting the table or clearing away the dishes. Get the children to attach their index card to the bag of soup mix using sticky tape and give them to their mums as Mother's Day gifts.

SAY: **Giving back to our mums is one way we honour our parents, just like God tells us to do. Let this Mother's Day be a reminder for you to help and honour your mum—all year round.**

Extra-special FACT

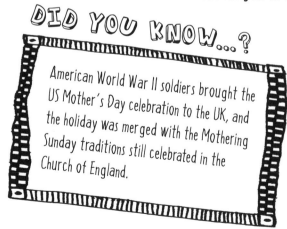

DID YOU KNOW...?

American World War II soldiers brought the US Mother's Day celebration to the UK, and the holiday was merged with the Mothering Sunday traditions still celebrated in the Church of England.

# My amazing mum

BEST All Ages FOR

*Children work together to discover how amazing mums are.*

## PROPS

• no props needed

## CAST

• Leader

## BEHIND THE SCENES

This interactive sketch involves children getting into groups of four, then using movement and mime. It works best if the audience has space to move about the room without chairs or tables obstructing them.

# Action!

➡ *The leader comes out to centre stage and gathers the audience into groups of four.*

## LEADER

My mum is amazing. Mums aren't perfect, true, and they make lots of mistakes, like everyone else. But they do a lot for us. In fact, without mums or women who serve as mums, none of us would even be here. Our clothes wouldn't match, we'd miss football practice and we'd eat chips for every meal. And more than just doing stuff, I know *my* amazing mum means a whole lot more. First, she's honest. I know I can count on my mum being honest and true. In your groups, using all of your hands, come up with a maths problem you know is true.

➡ *Show the children the example '1 + 1 = 2' by using fingers for the numbers and to make the plus and equals signs.*

## LEADER

And my amazing mum is honourable! That means she does what's right, and she knows the difference between what's right and what's wrong. In your groups, I'd like some of you to show me how to stand up tall the right way, and some to show me an opposite—or wrong—way to stand up tall.

➡ *Encourage the children to get really wacky with their stances. After a few seconds, ask them to switch who's doing normal and wacky stances.*

## LEADER

And my amazing mum is just! 'Just' means she's fair. Face someone in your group and show that person what your face looks like when things are unfair.

➡ *Allow about 10 seconds for this. Then continue.*

## LEADER

My mum is also very, very lovely. I think she's so pretty! Right now, walk around the room as if you were the prettiest person in here.

➡ *Allow about 20 seconds for the children to do this. Then continue.*

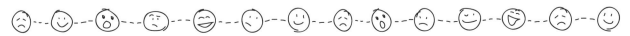

## LEADER

She's also kind. That means she talks nicely about people and tells everyone when I do something good. In your groups, turn to someone and talk about a time your mum told people about something you did well.

➡ *Allow about two minutes for the children to talk. Then continue.*

## LEADER

And last of all, my mum's heart is SO big and loving. My mum loves me and lets me know this every day. In your groups, on the ground, use your bodies to create the biggest heart shape you can.

➡ *Allow about one minute for this. Then conclude the sketch with the last line.*

## LEADER

So when I think about my mum, I'm going to think about her as true, honourable, just, lovely, kind and loving.

# I love you, yes I do

BEST
Preschool
FOR

*Children can thank their mums with these simple lyrics, set to the tune of 'Frère Jacques'.*

**SCRIPTURE**

Exodus 20:12

## Sing it!

**Special mummy, special mummy,**

*(hold out right hand and then left hand)*

**I love you, yes I do!**

*(place right hand on heart; then place left hand on heart)*

**On this day you'll know it,**

*(point a finger to the side of your head)*

**'Cause I'll really show it.**

*(hold your arms out wide to the sides)*

**I love you, yes I do!**

*(place right hand on heart; then place left hand on heart)*

Extra-special
FACTS

### DID YOU KNOW...?

American Anna Jarvis loved her mother. Anna watched her mum accomplish amazing things—founding clubs to help mothers in five US cities, working tirelessly to improve conditions at factories for women, and clothing and bandaging soldiers from both sides in the American Civil War. On 12 May 1907, two years after her mother's death, Anna held a memorial to her mother and started a campaign to make 'Mother's Day' a nationally recognised holiday in the US. She finally succeeded seven years later in 1914.

### DID YOU KNOW...?

After successfully creating the holiday, Anna found that the day she had envisioned, one of reflection and quiet prayers of thanks for all that mothers do, was becoming something completely different. She filed a lawsuit to stop the over-commercialisation of Mother's Day... which she lost.

# God gave me a mother

*Children can thank God for their mums with these simple lyrics, set to the tune of 'On top of Old Smokey'.*

**SCRIPTURE**

Exodus 20:12

## Sing it!

**For when I am lonely,**
  *(cup your hands around your eyes, as if looking for someone)*
**When I hurt my knee,**
  *(hold one knee)*
**God gave me a mother,**
  *(put hands over heart)*
**To take care of me.**
  *(hold up both hands)*

**She gives me some kisses,**
  *('throw' kisses with both hands)*
**She gives me some love.**
  *(wrap your arms around yourself)*
**God gave me a mother,**
  *(put hands over heart)*
**Whom I really love.**
  *(hold up both hands)*

Extra-special FACT

## DID YOU KNOW...?

Mother's Day is a big occasion in Mexico. On 10 May, churches join the celebration with a special service: an orchestra plays the traditional Mexican celebration song 'Las Mananitas' and church members feast on 'tamales' and 'atole'—a drink that typically includes 'masa' (coarsely ground maize), water, 'piloncillo' (unrefined whole cane sugar), cinnamon, vanilla and sometimes chocolate.

# Mum's helping hands

**BEST Primary Age FOR**

*Encourage the mums of your community by lightening their load.*

**SCRIPTURE**

1 Thessalonians 5:11

**WHAT YOU'LL NEED**

- Bible
- plain paper
- pencils
- thick, black felt-tip pens
- cookie cutters in various shapes and sizes
- sugar paper
- stickers
- hole punches
- wool
- four-packs of crayons

## The experience

Read aloud 1 Thessalonians 5:11. <u>SAY:</u> **Most mums have their hands full, literally, with children, so we're going to give the mums in our community a helping hand and encourage them this Mother's Day.** Ask the children to make colouring books to help mums keep their children occupied while waiting for appointments.

**1.** Get the children to trace cookie-cutter shapes on to paper with a pencil and then retrace the line with a thick, black felt-tip pen. Let each child make several pages.

**2.** For the cover of the colouring book, trace the children's hands in the centre of a piece of sugar paper.

**3.** Let the children decorate the covers with stickers and a title, such as 'Mum's Helping Hand'.

**4.** Add a note from your church on the back cover, saying 'Made by' and your church's name.

**5.** Help the children to punch a hole in one corner of each colouring page and then tie the pages together with wool.

**6.** Include a four-pack of crayons. (You can purchase these online, or you can divide up a larger box into home-made four-packs. Just wrap a rubber band around them and attach them to the cover with sticky tape.)

**7.** Distribute the colouring books to local doctors' surgeries for their waiting rooms, or make them available at the back of church for younger children.

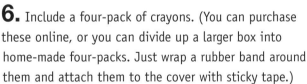

YOUR A SPECIAL DAD
HAPPY FATHER'S DAY
#1 DAD

**Bible Focus**
**Mr Fix-it**
*page 68*

**Craft**
**Peek-a-boo for dad**
*page 69*

**Game**
**Feats of strength**
*page 70*

**Snack**
**Our Father**
*page 71*

**Sketch**
**Role reversal**
*page 72*

**Song**
**I've got a Father**
*page 75*

**Outreach**
**Treasure ties**
*page 76*

Throughout the Bible, God calls himself our Father. That means every one of us has a father who loves and cares for us and who wants to be a big part of our lives. And God gave us a really special gift, too: dads or other special men who care about us and make a difference in our lives. With these Father's Day activities, children will appreciate their earthly fathers and special men who serve as fathers, and they'll learn that we all share the most gentle, wonderful Father we could ever imagine!

# Mr Fix-it

BEST
All Ages
FOR

Children learn that we all have a compassionate heavenly Father.

### SCRIPTURE

Psalm 103:13

### WHAT YOU'LL NEED

- Bible
- hammer
- nails
- duct tape
- scissors
- large sheet of card
- felt-tip pens

## The experience

SAY: **Let's talk about dads. Lots of dads make things and fix stuff—broken toilets, wobbly chairs, leaky taps.**

Hold up a hammer and nails and ASK:

- **What things could we make or fix with these?**

Hold up a roll of duct tape and ASK:

- **What could we make or fix with this?**
- **Why do you think some fix-it jobs need duct tape and some need a hammer and nails?**
- **Why do dads need to be tough sometimes and at other times tender and caring?**

SAY: **Dads might use duct tape, glue, nails or even bandages to fix things. And the Bible tells us we _all_ have a Father who's great at fixing things—even the really big things—and who wants to help us. That's because God is a father to us.**

Read aloud Psalm 103:13.

ASK: **How do you think God is like or unlike a dad?**

- **What kinds of things can God fix in our lives?**

Hold up the hammer and SAY: **It's good to remember God's power and might.** Hold up the duct tape. **But don't forget that God is tender, gentle and compassionate to us. The duct tape is powerful.** Cut off a piece of duct tape and let a few children try to pull it apart as if they're playing tug of war. **But it's also soft and doesn't break anything.** Let everyone touch the non-sticky side of the tape to feel how soft and smooth it is.

SAY: **Let's use this duct tape to show how much we love God.**

Use the duct tape to write 'DAD' on the large sheet of card. (If you have lots of children, make multiple posters.) Let the children write words of thanks to God on the poster, as a prayer of praise to their gentle and compassionate heavenly Father.

# Peek-a-boo for dad

BEST for All Ages

*Children reveal the ways dads stay busy to help them.*

## SCRIPTURE

Proverbs 10:1

## WHAT YOU'LL NEED

- Bible
- 1 copy per child of 'Peek-a-boo for dad symbols' handout on page 121, on coloured card
- 1 copy per child of 'Father's Day symbols' handout on page 120, on white paper or card
- scissors
- glue sticks
- felt-tip pens or crayons

## The experience

Before the children arrive, copy the handout on page 120 on to paper or card, and cut out the shapes. Copy the handout on page 121 on to card, and cut along three sides of each square, so there are nine flaps. Repeat until there are enough handouts for each child.

<u>SAY:</u> **Father's Day is a time to celebrate the dads in our lives—our own dads, our grandfathers and uncles, and other men in our lives who make a difference. Let's hear what the Bible has to say about how God wants us to treat those men.**

Read Proverbs 10:1.

<u>ASK:</u> **Based on this verse, what do you think you can do to bring joy to your dad?**

<u>SAY:</u> **Fathers in the Bible did all kinds of things with their sons and daughters. They travelled together. They ate together. They herded sheep together. They fished together. They sat around the fire together. They built things together. Jesus' father, Joseph, taught him all about carpentry.**

<u>ASK:</u> **What kinds of things do you do with your dad?**

<u>SAY:</u> **Let's show our dads or the special men in our lives how great they are at loving us and helping us in all kinds of ways.** Spread the cut-outs of the symbols on the workspace, and distribute the card with flaps cut out. **Take a look at all these pictures and choose the ones that remind you of your dad or another special man. Then glue each one to the outside of a flap. On the inside of the flap, draw or write a message that relates to that picture.**

When the children have finished, <u>SAY:</u> **Give your dad this craft and show him each flap as you thank him for all he does for you.**

# Feats of strength

*The children experience a series of interactive challenges that test their strength—and get them talking about how strong their dads really are.*

## WHAT YOU'LL NEED

- ideally, soft carpeting or floor mats
- no other supplies needed

## The experience

Get the children to form pairs. <u>SAY</u>: **We're going to discover how strong you are by trying a series of challenges. Your first challenge? One-legged elbow wrestling!** Ask partners to interlock their right elbows and hold one foot off the ground at the same time. When you say 'Go,' the children will attempt to push their partners off balance. The challenge ends when the first person in each pair has to put his or her foot down to keep them from falling. (With this and the following challenges, check that the pushing and pulling don't become aggressive, and make sure that the pairs are evenly matched.)

Ask the children to switch partners.

<u>SAY</u>: **Next? Flat-bottomed back wrestling!** Ask the children to sit on the floor, back-to-back and elbows interlocked, with their knees raised close to the chest. **On 'Go,' the first person to get his or her partner's right shoulder to touch the ground wins. Ready, go!** Allow time.

Ask the children to switch partners again.

<u>SAY</u>: **Last? The toe-to-toe hand pull!** Get the children to sit on the floor facing their partners with toes touching. <u>SAY</u>: **Interlink both your hands with your partner's hands (do not yank!) On 'Go,' try to lift your partner off the ground by pulling his or her hands. The challenge is over when one person leaves the ground. Ready, go!** Allow time.

Once the children have completed all three challenges, encourage them to share which events they were strongest in. Applaud everyone's efforts.

<u>ASK</u>: **Talk about a time when you felt strong.**

- **Other than physical strength, in what ways are people strong?**

- **Who's the strongest person you know—and what makes that person so strong?**

<u>SAY</u>: **Father's Day is a day when we recognise all the great things about our dads, including their physical, emotional, mental and spiritual strength. Father's Day is also a day to recognise that we have an amazing, strong and powerful Father in heaven—God, who loves us very much and is stronger than anyone.**

Close in prayer, thanking God for our fathers and for being our Father.

# Snack

# Our Father

BEST
All Ages
FOR

*The children eat snacks that help them understand how special fathers are—including our heavenly Father.*

### SCRIPTURE

Genesis 17:4;
Matthew 6:9;
Romans 8:15–16

ALLERGY
See
p. 7
ALERT

### WHAT YOU'LL NEED

- Bible
- selection of different fruits, washed and chopped
- star-shaped sweets such as Milky Way Magic Stars®
- wafers or Rich Tea biscuits
- icing
- plastic knives

## The experience

Ask the children to wash their hands.

SAY: **Father's Day is a time to celebrate the dads in our lives and to remember God, too. Did you know there are more than 1000 verses about fathers in the Bible? We're going to look at three of them and eat a snack that helps us understand each one.**

**The first verse is from the Old Testament. God tells Abraham he has big plans for him.** Invite a child to read Genesis 17:4. Hand out the fruit. **There are many different kinds of fruit, and that can remind us of the many children Abraham had. Just think—some of us might be Abraham's great-great-great-great-great-times-a-lot-grandchildren!** Let the children eat their fruit.

ASK: **What's something special you can think of about your grandpa or your great-grandpa?**

SAY: **Here's another verse where Jesus teaches us how to pray.** Read Matthew 6:9. **When Jesus taught his followers to pray, he started by calling God 'Our Father'. And Jesus recognised that God was our Father in heaven.** Distribute star-shaped sweets. **These sweets remind us of the stars in the sky, which help us remember just how big and amazing God is.** Let the children eat their sweets.

ASK: **Tell us about one way God has shown you how big he is.**

SAY: **Here's the last verse.** Read Romans 8:15–16. *Abba* **is a special Greek word that children could use to talk to their fathers. It's very personal, like our word 'daddy'.** Distribute the wafers or Rich Tea biscuits, icing and plastic knives. **Stick two biscuits together with icing to remember just how close you are to God.** Let the children eat their biscuits.

ASK: **How is God like your daddy?**

• **Why do you think God wants us to feel so close to him?**

SAY: **This Father's Day, remember to thank your dad or someone who loves you like a dad for the way he shows you God's love. And remember that all of us—even people whose dads aren't with them—have a heavenly Father who loves us very much.**

# Role reversal

*A dad and his son switch roles.*

**SCRIPTURE**

Galatians 4:6

**PROPS**

• no supplies needed

**CAST**

• Dad
• Son

**BEHIND THE SCENES**

The stage can be empty, just dad and son in the centre. Both parts need to be cast with people who are animated, and the dialogue can be spoken rather quickly—but still clearly so the audience can understand.

 *Action!*

→ *Dad and son are centre stage.*

**DAD**

Hi, son.

**SON**

Hi, Dad.

**DAD**

How are you doing?

**SON**

Can't complain. You?

**DAD**

Oh, you know. Good days, bad days. I'm hanging in there.

**SON**

I have a question.

**DAD**

OK.

**SON**

What's it like to be a dad?

**DAD**

Oh! Um... I was thinking you were going to ask me how to kick a football or something...

**SON**

Because I want to be a good one.

**DAD**

You do, eh?

**SON**

Yep.

**DAD**

Well... maybe the best way is for you to just be one yourself.

 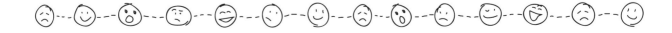

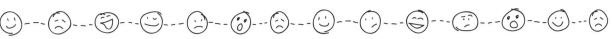
**SON**

Wait. What? I'm going to be a dad?

**DAD**

No, no, just pretend to be one. You know, switch roles.

**SON**

Like, you're the kid and I'm the dad?

**DAD**

Yep!

**SON**

Cool! Go to your room!

**DAD**

Wait, I...

**SON**

Clean up your mess!

**DAD**

Hang on just a...

**SON**

I'm going to complain about my boss!

**DAD**

Now, wait a second. There's more to being a dad than shouting orders and telling people what to do.

**SON**

There is?

**DAD**

Yes. Let's pretend. *(Pretends to be hurt)* Ow! Ow! *(Wincing)* I twisted my ankle.

**SON**

Walk it off.

**DAD**

Hey! I'm serious here.

**SON**

OK, let me take a look.

**DAD**

Ow! It hurts. Be careful.

**SON**

Let me see. Hmm. Dear Lord, I pray for my son's ankle...

**DAD**

Wait. What are you doing?

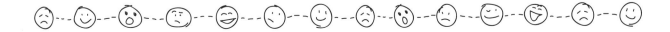

**SON**

Praying. It's what you do when I'm hurt.

**DAD**

I do?

**SON**

Yep.

**DAD**

*(Smiles)* **OK, how about this one?**
*(Switching gears to more animated)* **Dad! Dad, can we play a game?**

**SON**

Can't. Football's on.

**DAD**

Hey, I'm serious here!

**SON**

OK, OK. Tell you what. Let's go outside, just you and me, and spend some quality time together. How about that?

**DAD**

I said that?

**SON**

Yep. Yesterday.

**DAD**

Wow. I'm a great dad.

**SON**

Yeah. You are. So basically, all I have to do to be a good dad is to... do what you do.

**DAD**

Yeah. I guess so. So can we switch back now?

**SON**

No. I'm going to take the car for a drive.

➡ *He turns and quickly starts to exit.*

**DAD**

Hey! Bad dad! I mean, son! Get back here!

BEST Preschool FOR

# I've got a Father

Extra-special FACTS

*A song about God our Father, sung to the tune of 'I'm a little teapot'.*

**SCRIPTURE**

1 John 3:1

## Sing it!

**I've got a Father,**

*(point thumb to chest, indicating 'me')*

**Big and strong.**

*(show muscles)*

**He loves me**

*(put your hand over your heart)*

**My whole life long.**

*(point left, centre, right.)*

**When I need a hand,**

*(hold out right hand)*

**Just hear me shout:**

*(hold hands up to mouth and shout the word 'shout')*

**My God in heaven**

*(point up)*

**Can help me out!**

*(point thumb to chest, indicating 'me')*

### DID YOU KNOW...?

American Sonora Smart Dodd conceived the idea of Father's Day in Spokane, Washington, while listening to a Mother's Day sermon in 1909. Dodd (known in the US as 'the mother of Father's Day') wanted a day to honour her father, William Smart, a widowed Civil War veteran who single-handedly raised his six children on a farm.

### DID YOU KNOW...?

In most languages, regardless of the pronunciation of the actual word in that language, small children first call their fathers 'da-da'—the origin of the English word 'dad'.

# Treasure ties

*Show kindness to the dads in your community with these fun tie bookmarks.*

**SCRIPTURE**

Proverbs 3:3

**WHAT YOU'LL NEED**

- Bible
- coloured card
- adhesive Velcro® strips
- foam board
- felt-tip pens
- 'Treasure ties' handout on page 122
- scissors

## The experience

Copy the 'Treasure ties' handout on to various colours of card, and cut out the tie shapes.

<u>SAY:</u> **Today's dads can get bogged down by worries and stress over providing for their families and working long hours. They need a little encouragement!** Read Proverbs 3:3. **Let's tie kindness around the necks of the dads in our community with a fun poster!** (Note that not all Bible translations use the word 'kindness' in Proverbs 3:3, so for this activity try to read from a version that does, such as the New Living Translation.)

Give the children felt-tip pens to decorate the tie shapes with fun patterns, and ask them to write encouraging messages on each tie, such as, 'We're glad you're a dad!' or 'Dads are great!'

As the children work, stick a number of pieces of Velcro® on each piece of foam board, leaving room to stick a tie to each piece. Write, 'Dads: Please take a bookmark tie!' on the foam board. Help the children to attach a piece of Velcro® to the upper back of each tie and stick each tie on to the foam board.

Ask places around your local community if they will display the boards, so dads can take tie bookmarks and feel appreciated.

**Extra-special FACT**

**DID YOU KNOW...?**

Around 4000 years ago, a Babylonian youth named Elmesu carved a card out of clay to wish his father good health and long life.

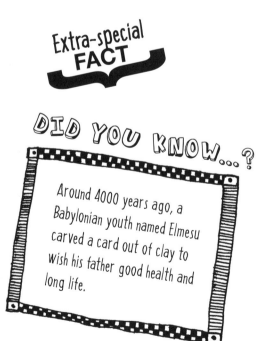

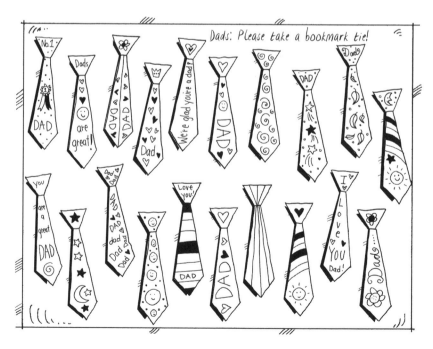

# Harvest

**W**hen God created the world, he told people to take part in caring for it. Genesis 1:28 tells us to rule over the earth. Although harvest is mainly a time to thank God for his provision for us, we can also celebrate this festival as people who love God and want to fulfil his call to care for his creation. These activities will help children understand why and how we can take care of God's earth.

# Handle with care

 BEST Primary Age FOR

*Children practise caring for God's creation.*

**SCRIPTURE**

Genesis 1:28–30

**WHAT YOU'LL NEED**

• Bible
• hard-boiled egg, washed in soapy water and then treated with hand sanitiser prior to use. (It may be wise to have some spare eggs in case of breakages.)
• paper towels

## The experience

SAY: **The Bible tells us God made the entire world—every rock, tree, giraffe and dung beetle.**

ASK: **How would you describe the world God made?**

SAY: **After God made the earth, he gave people a *really* important job. Let's see what that was.** Read aloud Genesis 1:28–30.

ASK: **Explain whether you still think that's our job today.**

• **How do people do that job today?**

Hold up the egg. SAY: **Let's pretend that this egg is the** [*use the words the children came up with to describe the world*] **world God made. And it's up to us to take care of it.**

Get the children to stand in a circle. (Check if any children have egg allergies—if they do, they'll have to sit out of this activity.) Demonstrate how to hold the egg one foot above the hand of the person to your left. Drop the egg into that person's open palm. Pass the egg carefully around the circle, dropping it into each person's hand. (It's OK if the egg breaks—you'll make an even stronger point! Just use paper towels to clean it up and make sure the children wash their hands.) Set the egg aside when it returns.

ASK: **What were you feeling as you passed the egg?**

• **How did those feelings impact the way you handled the egg?**

• **How is this experience like or unlike taking care of the earth God gave us?**

SAY: **At harvest time, it's good to remind ourselves of our responsibility to take care of God's world. When we love God, we can show our love for him by taking care of what he created. So every time you recycle, pick up rubbish or turn off a light, you're doing a job God gave especially to you.**

△ ▽ △ ▽ △ ▽ △ ▽ **Craft** ▽ △ ▽ △ ▽ △ ▽ △ ▽

# Salvage and recycle

**BEST All Ages FOR**

*Clean up your resources cupboard and recycle leftovers with this easy craft.*

**SCRIPTURE**

2 Corinthians 5:17

**WHAT YOU'LL NEED**

- Bible
- green paper plates
- blue modelling dough
- scissors
- glue
- various recyclables and extra craft supplies, including old (rust-free) nuts and bolts, bottle tops, coloured craft sticks, pompom balls, pipe cleaners and more
- felt-tip pens

## The experience

SAY: **This week we're celebrating harvest, a time when we can remind ourselves of our responsibility to look after God's earth. One thing we can do to care for the earth is recycle. That helps make the earth's resources last longer. Recycling goes back pretty far in history; in fact, the Bible says Jesus recycled us!**

Read 2 Corinthians 5:17.

ASK: **What do you think are some old things Jesus gets rid of in us?**

• **How has Jesus transformed you into something amazing?**

SAY: **Today we're going to recycle and repurpose old things to make a new creation.**

Get the children to roll the modelling dough into a ball and press it flat on to the centre of the plate. Then they can create their salvage sculptures by arranging supplies into the modelling dough. (Watch that younger children don't put the smaller items into their mouths.) Ask or help the children to write, 'The old life is gone; a new life has begun!' on their plates.

SAY: **This harvest time, remember to care for the earth the way Jesus cares for each of us—by recycling the old into something creative and new!**

△ ▽ △ ▽ △ ▽ △ ▽ △ ▽ △ ▽ △ ▽ △ ▽ △

# Creation sculptures

*Children are the sculptures in this creatively interactive game.*

**SCRIPTURE**

Genesis 2:9–12, 15

**WHAT YOU'LL NEED**

• Bible

## The experience

SAY: **God created an entire world full of things—like trees, water and stones—that we use to make *other* things that help us live. Listen.**

Read Genesis 2:9–12.

ASK: **What kinds of things do people make with trees, water or stones?**

SAY: **Today, we're going to make sculptures using something else God made—us! Let's play creation sculptures.**

Get the children to sit in a circle, leaving a good-sized space in the middle. Ask three children to stand in the centre of the circle and, whispering so the rest of the circle can't hear, ask them to discuss a position they can freeze in that shows something in God's creation. For example, one child might crouch down on all

fours, and another might freeze behind that person with an arm extended to look like the trunk of an elephant. Encourage the children to think creatively and be willing to laugh and have fun with it.

Once the three children have decided and posed, ask the other children in the circle to call out what part of creation they think the sculpture represents. Once someone guesses correctly, read Genesis 2:15. Then ask the children to call out different ways to protect or take care of the part of creation that the creation sculpture represented. Continue playing as time allows so each child has a chance to pose in a creation sculpture.

ASK: **What's one of your favourite things in all of God's creation?**

• **Talk about a time when you saw God's creation treated poorly.**

• **What can you do to protect and take care of what God made?**

SAY: **Harvest is a time when we can celebrate everything God has made. We can stop to appreciate God's creation and learn ways to protect and keep those things safe. We can pick up rubbish, recycle rather than throw away, or plant a tree as we remember that God created everything.**

# Seven days to praise

*Children gobble up goodies as they praise God for his amazing creation.*

**SCRIPTURE**

Psalm 148:3–5; Genesis 1:1 — 2:4a

**WHAT YOU'LL NEED**

- Bible
- white paper place mats
- felt-tip pens
- light and dark coloured cake sprinkles, mixed together
- clear plastic cups
- milk
- chocolate syrup
- spoons
- fruit pieces
- oranges, sliced
- cheese, cut in circles
- fish-shaped snacks (for example, from Burton's Fish 'n' Chips™ snack bags)
- animal biscuits
- marshmallows

## The experience

Ask the children to wash their hands.

SAY: **Harvest is a time to think about God's amazing creation.** Read Psalm 148:3–5. **God's creation praises him—even the things that can't move or talk. And we can praise him for his creation, too. Let's make a snack to explore some of the things God created. But first, draw seven boxes on your place mats.**

Distribute place mats and felt-tip pens, and allow time for the children to draw boxes.

SAY: **On the first day of creation, God separated light and darkness.** Spoon some sprinkles on to the first box on their place mats. **Separate your light and dark sprinkles as you talk about what you love about light or darkness.**

SAY: **Next, God separated the water and the sky. A little chocolate milk can help us think through what God did.** Distribute glasses of milk, and

then add chocolate syrup. Note how the chocolate stays separate at the bottom when it's not mixed in with the milk. **It's a good thing God split the sky and the water—what a mess it would be if the two were all mixed together! But our milk will taste better mixed up.** Distribute spoons. **Stir your milk as you share something you love about the sky and something you love about the water.** Ask the children to place their cups in the second box on their place mats.

SAY: **Then God made the land and the seas. And on the land, he created plants and trees. That includes fruit that grows on plants and trees! Let's put some fruit pieces in our next box as we praise God for our favourite kind of fruit or vegetable.** Distribute the fruit.

SAY: **Next, God created the sun, moon and stars. Let's put an orange-slice sun and a cheese moon in our fourth box. Then share one thing you love about the things God made to light up the sky.** Distribute orange slices and cheese circles.

SAY: **Then God filled the sky with birds and the waters with fish. Let's get a few fish for our fifth box as you talk about your favourite birds and fish.** Distribute fish-shaped snacks.

SAY: **Next, God put animals and people on the land. As you choose a couple of animal biscuits for box six, praise God for your favourite animal.** Distribute animal biscuits.

SAY: **On the last day of creation, God rested. Let's put a marshmallow pillow in box seven to remind us of that day.** Distribute marshmallows.

SAY: **After God created everything, he said it was very good. Let's see how good our snack is! As you eat, call out words that describe God's wonderful creation.**

# Clean earth

BEST For All Ages

*A sketch about how we sometimes mistreat God's earth.*

### SCRIPTURE

Genesis 1:31

### PROPS

- chair or stool
- sign to be hung around someone's neck that reads 'EARTH'
- empty disposable coffee cup
- piece of chewing gum
- plastic bag with crumpled-up paper and sweet wrappers in it
- bin bag
- sponge
- pen

### CAST

- EARTH, dressed in blue and white, with a sign that reads 'EARTH' around his or her neck
- Person One, chewing a piece of gum and holding a coffee cup
- Person Two, carrying a plastic bag with crumpled-up paper and sweet wrappers
- Child, carrying a bin bag, a sponge and a pen

### BEHIND THE SCENES

This is a simple sketch, with an easy set-up and no dialogue. The actor playing EARTH will use very animated facial expressions.

## Action!

➜ The sketch begins with EARTH seated centre stage, looking down at the sign that reads 'EARTH' and smiling.

Person One walks on stage chewing gum and carrying a disposable coffee cup. He takes out his chewing gum and sticks it on to EARTH's sign. He takes one last sip of his coffee and then throws the cup into EARTH's lap. EARTH's smile fades a little—it's as though EARTH is trying to make the best of it but is a bit embarrassed now.

Person Two enters with a plastic bag slung over her shoulder. She walks over to EARTH and pulls out crumpled-up papers and sweet wrappers, dropping them on EARTH's lap. EARTH doesn't react (except to close their eyes). Person Two does this a few times, making sure EARTH is covered. Then she throws the empty plastic bag at EARTH and turns and exits.

EARTH sits—dirty, messy and looking as sad as possible.

After a long pause, a child enters. She's carrying a bin bag and a sponge. As she interacts with EARTH, she is gentle and careful, treating EARTH very tenderly. She starts by taking the rubbish off and putting it in her bin bag. One piece at a time, she puts the rubbish in her bag. She makes a face when she reaches the chewing gum, and uses the discarded plastic bag as a glove to take it off.

Next, she goes around to EARTH's back and pretends to clean it, using the sponge. She pulls more rubbish off and puts it in the bin bag. Finally, she takes off the sign marked 'EARTH', writes the words 'Take care of the' above the word 'EARTH' and rehangs the sign around EARTH's neck.

The child exits, and as she does, EARTH springs to life, picks up the sign and smiles gratefully.

# God has given us this world

**BEST All Ages FOR**

Children learn about God's gift of creation through this descriptive song set to the tune of 'Twinkle, twinkle, little star'.

**SCRIPTURE**

Genesis 1

## Sing it!

**Every boy and every girl,**

*(point to other children)*

**God has given us this world,**

*(fold hands across chest)*

**Oceans deep and great big sky,**

*(hands down as if putting them in water; then hands stretched high and wide)*

**Forests green and mountains high,**

*(arms held upright like trees; then touch hands to form a 'mountain' shape)*

**Every boy and every girl,**

*(point to other children)*

**Let's take care of God's big world.**

*(hold hands with your neighbour)*

**Extra-special FACTS**

### DID YOU KNOW...?

The earth's estimated weight is 5,972,000,000,000,000,000,000 metric tons. Plus, the earth isn't a perfect sphere. The earth's rotation causes it to bulge around the equator.

### DID YOU KNOW...?

Scientists estimate that there could be approximately 8.7 million species on the earth. According to the journal 'PLoS Biology', a whopping 86% of all species on land and 91% of those in the seas have yet to be discovered.

# Clean-up committee

BEST **Juniors** FOR

*Children help restore beauty to God's creation.*

**SCRIPTURE**

Psalm 24:1

**WHAT YOU'LL NEED**

- Bible
- work gloves for each child
- bin bags

## The experience

Plan to pick up cans, bottles and other litter in your community. Choose a section of town, a park or several areas, depending on the size of your group, to target for the clean-up. If necessary form separate groups, with adult leaders as needed. Make sure the children are aware of potentially dangerous items that they shouldn't pick up (such as broken glass, discarded needles, used chewing gum, and so on) and supervise them carefully during the clean-up.

Begin the session by reading Psalm 24:1.

<u>SAY:</u> **In the beginning, God gave Adam care over all the earth. Harvest is a good time to acknowledge God as Creator and honour him by taking care of what he made.**

Help the children to clean up the designated area. Separate rubbish from recyclables.

Afterwards, encourage the children to reflect on the experience. Ask them what it was like to pick up other people's rubbish. Close with a prayer, thanking God for his creation and asking him to help us remember to take care of it.

Extra-special
**FACT**

**DID YOU KNOW...?**

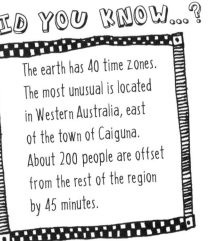

The earth has 40 time zones. The most unusual is located in Western Australia, east of the town of Caiguna. About 200 people are offset from the rest of the region by 45 minutes.

**TRICK or TREAT**

# Halloween

COSTUME Boo

H alloween is much debated among Christians. Many have practical concerns about the safety of trick-or-treating. Others find it a disturbing event for Christians to take part in. While the festival has its pagan origins (later redeemed by the Church), it still offers a great opportunity to teach children important truths. Use these activities to teach children about discerning good and evil and conquering death with life in Jesus.

# Good or evil?

BEST
Primary Age
FOR

*Good or evil? Children learn to discern between the two with this optical illusion.*

### SCRIPTURE

Matthew 7:15; Romans 12:21

### WHAT YOU'LL NEED

• copy of the 'Optical illusion' handout on page 123 for each child (use thin paper)

## The experience

Give each child a copy of the 'Optical illusion' handout. Tell them they have five seconds to look at the page, and when you call time, they can call out the word they see.

SAY: **There are lots of things that look harmless or even good. Turn your paper over and hold it up to the light. See if you can read another word.** Help the children look inside the white part of the letters to read the word 'evil'.

SAY: **Sometimes it's hard to tell the difference between good and evil. Sometimes, the devil makes evil look like it's good. But when we hold our decisions up to the light of God's word, we see the truth about what's good and what's not.**

ASK: **Talk about someone or something you pretended to be either for Halloween or just for fun.**

SAY: **At Halloween, lots of people dress up in costumes and pretend to be someone or something else. That can be a fun way to celebrate! But Jesus warned us in real life about evil people who pretend to be good. They aren't just having fun.** Read aloud Matthew 7:15. **Sometimes people tell lies about Jesus or do wrong things, but they make it appear to be good. It's a bit like wearing a costume, only it can hurt God and other people.**

ASK: **How is pretending at Halloween different from someone pretending to be good when he or she really isn't?**

• **Without naming names, talk about someone who seemed nice at first, but ended up not being so nice.**

SAY: **At Halloween, it's obvious when people are dressed in a costume. You probably didn't believe there was a real witch or skeleton walking down your street! With God's help, telling the difference between good and evil is also possible. It can be just like holding your paper up to the light. And when we can tell good and evil apart, here's what can happen.** Ask a child to read Romans 12:21 aloud to the group.

ASK: **What does it mean to you to conquer evil by doing good?**

• **What are some ways that God turns bad things into good?**

• **How can you tell which parts of Halloween are good and which are bad?**

SAY: **At Halloween it's good to remember all the great things God does for us and to celebrate all the goodness in the world. The Bible tells us that God has conquered evil with good. That's something to celebrate!**

# Glowing slime

*This gooey, slimy craft helps children discover how God holds them firmly.*

**SCRIPTURE**

1 John 5:18; Matthew 5:16

**WHAT YOU'LL NEED**

- Bible
- 4 cups of cornflour
- 2 cups of warm water
- 4–6 tablespoons of glow-in-the-dark craft paint (available at most craft stores)
- food colouring (optional)
- spoons
- cups and spoons for measuring
- large bowl
- resealable bags
- permanent markers
- aprons
- mats or boards for kneading

## The experience

**1.** Get one child to pour the cornflour into a bowl (you can use less cornflour to produce a more watery slime), then ask another child to add the water to the bowl.

**2.** Choose another child to stir the mixture well.

**3.** Ask other children to add the craft paint, and to continue stirring until the desired consistency is achieved.

**4.** You can also add drops of food colouring to change the colour of the slime, but the food colouring may make the slime glow a little less.

**5.** Give each child some of the slime and get them to knead it until it feels dry. (Don't worry about excess water remaining in the bowl.) The more the children play with the slime, the firmer and less sticky it will become.

While the children play, SAY: **Imagine you're the slime. Slime is slippery and hard to hold on to. That's a bit like how the devil tries to hold on to us: we slip right out of his fingers!**

Read aloud 1 John 5:18.

ASK: **How does the way God holds us compare with how you hold your slime?**

• **What does it mean to you that 'God's children do not make a practice of sinning'?** (Adapt the wording of this question according to the Bible version you are using.)

SAY: **When God holds us, he helps us to avoid sin and stay out of the devil's grasp. And something else happens to us.** Read aloud Matthew 5:16. Turn out the lights to reveal the glowing slime.

SAY: **At Halloween, it can be easy to focus on evil, scary things. But this Halloween, remember that God is holding your hand, helping you shine with good deeds that show other people how awesome God is.**

Pass out resealable bags and permanent markers, and let the children decorate their bags. Put each child's slime in the bag, and seal it tightly to keep it from evaporating. Clean up as needed and make sure the children wash their hands.

# Stomp!

*Children will have some foot-stomping, balloon-popping fun.*

**SCRIPTURE**

Romans 8:28

**WHAT YOU'LL NEED**

- Bible
- dark-coloured balloons
- wrapped sweets
- 60 cm lengths of string

## The experience

Before the children arrive, push one wrapped sweet inside each balloon. Inflate the balloons and tie them. Gather the children together. Give each child a balloon and a piece of string. Help them tie one end of the string to the balloon and the other end of the string to their ankle. Although the children might realise something is inside the balloons, don't tell them what it is.

SAY: **The object of this game is to pop everyone else's balloons by stomping on them—while keeping your own balloon from being popped. Once your balloon pops, stop where you are and gather the leftover pieces from your popped balloon. Ready? Go!**

*Tip* Dark-coloured balloons work better for this activity because the colour prevents children from seeing the sweets. If you don't have dark colours, use thicker balloons.

Play until only one person is left with an unpopped balloon—then get him or her to pop it. Once everyone's balloon is popped, ask the children to 'pop' their sweets in their mouths.

SAY: **Even though having your balloon popped seemed like a bad thing, what popped out of your balloon was a *good* thing. In life, bad things happen. It might seem like nothing good could *ever* come out of something bad. But here's good news: God can take what's bad and turn it around for good!**

Ask the children to find a partner to discuss the following questions.

ASK: **What were you thinking when your balloon popped and you discovered a treat inside?**

- **Talk about a time when something bad happened in your life.**

- **What good, if any, do you think came out of that bad thing?**

Read aloud Romans 8:28. SAY: **Halloween, 31 October, might seem to some like a 'bad day'. But as in our game, something good can come out of something bad. Halloween is a great time to meet and get to know your neighbours, and to tell people about Jesus. Jesus dying on the cross may have seemed like a bad thing— but *really* it was the most amazing thing ever. God took something bad and turned it into good, and he can do the same in our lives!**

Be aware that some children may be afraid of balloons popping.

Warning! To avoid choking hazards, do pick up pieces of any broken balloons promptly. Balloons may contain latex.

# Pumpkin pancake party

*Children learn how new life springs from death.*

## SCRIPTURE

Romans 6:11

## WHAT YOU'LL NEED

- Bible
- pancake ingredients (makes 12):
  * 100 g plain flour
  * 2 large eggs
  * 300 ml milk
- pumpkin purée
- cooking oil
- mixing bowl
- weighing scales
- measuring jug
- whisk/blender
- frying pan
- cooker (for adult use only)
- spatula
- plates
- forks

## The experience

At home, cut a pumpkin into chunks, peel the chunks then boil them until they are tender. Drain the water then purée the pumpkin and refrigerate it.

At the start of the session, get the children to wash their hands.

SAY: **One reason Halloween can be so scary is that it focuses a lot on death. People often dress up as things that symbolise death, like ghosts or skeletons. But as Christians, we don't need to fear death. This Halloween, let's see what death means for Christians.**

Invite the children to help you prepare the pancakes by measuring and mixing the ingredients. Whisk to a smooth batter. Cook the pancakes in a little cooking oil over a medium heat for one minute each side until golden, then serve them to the children with pumpkin purée. As you add the pumpkin, SAY: **This pumpkin comes from a real, live pumpkin that grew on a plant. The pumpkin died to become our snack. But we're taking a dead pumpkin and turning it into something wonderful—and yummy!**

As the children eat, read Romans 6:11.

ASK: **How does this verse make you think about death?**

• **What do you think it means to be dead to the power of sin?**

SAY: **Our pumpkin died, but it became something wonderful. That's like what Jesus does in our lives. Through Jesus, we're dead to the power of sin. And we're transformed into life in Jesus! You can celebrate the death of sin this Halloween by living for Jesus.**

# God's with Matt, too

*Matt's dad reminds him what to do when there's scary stuff around.*

## SCRIPTURE

Isaiah 41:13

## PROPS

• chair

## CAST

• Dad
• Matt
• Mum
• Noisemaker—someone who cues the audience to make noises

## BEHIND THE SCENES

This has a basic set-up of one chair at centre stage—and two actors who don't have any problem being over-theatrical. For the character of Matt, the bigger the reactions, the better! The Noisemaker should stand off to the side of the stage, 'unseen' by the actors on the stage but still in view of the audience.

# Action!

➡ *Matt is sitting in a chair. His knees are pulled up to his chest and his arms are wrapped around his legs. He is jumpy and scared, but we don't know why. He's looking around, seemingly terrified at the smallest things. Dad enters.*

## NOISEMAKER

*(Loudly whispers to the audience)* **Everyone, on the count of three, stamp your feet on the ground once. One, two, *three!***

➡ *As the audience stamps its feet, Matt jumps up, reacting to the sound. He's terrified, and runs behind the chair to hide. Matt's dad enters, looking around for Matt.*

## DAD

**Matt? You in here?** *(Looks around, but can't find him)* **Matt? It's bedtime.**

## NOISEMAKER

**He-he-he!** *(Then loudly whispers to the audience)* **On the count of three, everyone say, 'BUMP!' One, two, *three!***

➡ *At the audience's 'BUMP!' Matt comes out from behind the chair, screaming.*

## DAD

**Whoa, whoa! What's wrong? That was just Buster. He keeps running into the wall.**

## MATT

**No, that wasn't Buster. That was a monster. A big, huge, green, slimy monster with fangs coming out of its mouth and...**

## DAD

**Whoa, Matt, slow down. There are no monsters.**

**MATT**

I've seen them! Every time you turn out the lights, they're there!

**NOISEMAKER**

*(Loudly whispers to the audience)* **On the count of three, everyone say, 'CRASH!' and clap your hands together once. One, two, *three!***

➡ *At the audience's noise, Matt jumps into his dad's arms. He screams for an overly long time. After running out of air, Matt calms down and his dad sets him back on the ground.*

**MATT**

I may have got a little carried away that time.

**DAD**

Just a smidge.

**MATT**

That was Buster, too, wasn't it?

**DAD**

I'm guessing yes. *(Pauses)* **What's got into you, anyway? What are you so scared of?**

**MATT**

Every time I close my eyes I see monsters. There's a zombie cowboy in

my wardrobe and a fur-covered half-man, half-fly under my bed.

**DAD**

Well, why don't we check the wardrobe and look under the bed together?

**MATT**

It won't help. They're only here when I'm alone.

**DAD**

Did something happen to scare you?

**MATT**

If by 'something' you mean 'Halloween', then yes.

**DAD**

Ah, it's that time of year again, isn't it? You're seeing scary stuff everywhere and it's got your brain working overtime.

**MATT**

*(Shrugs)* **I guess.**

**NOISEMAKER**

*(Loudly whispers to the audience)* **On the count of three, everyone whistle and make noises like the wind going through the trees. One, two, *three!***

➡ *At the audience's noises, Matt stiffens, grabs hold of his dad and looks around, really scared.*

## DAD

It's OK, it's OK. It's just the wind. Matt, didn't we talk about this last year? Remember what we said?

## MATT

You said there's nothing to be afraid of. But that doesn't mean I agreed.

## DAD

Well, do you remember what else I said? That when you get scared...

## MATT

I should pray.

## DAD

Because...

## MATT

God's with me... so I don't need to be afraid.

## DAD

Son, there's all kinds of scary stuff around right now. The other day I saw a house with a skeleton sitting at the window. And Mr Jenkins has started wearing that gorilla costume again. If I didn't know better, I might be afraid myself.

## MATT

You?

## DAD

Yes, me. But even though I feel fear, I know I've got a great big God on my side.

➡ *Just then, Mum enters and taps Dad on the shoulder. He jumps and screams for 30 seconds straight. Mum and Matt stare at him until he finally runs out of air, looks at them and calms down.*

## MATT

God's with you, Dad.

## DAD

Thanks, son. I needed that.

## NOISEMAKER

*(Loudly whispers to the audience)* **On the count of three, everyone say, 'Ahhhh.' One, two, *three*!**

# Oh, God Almighty

**BEST Preschool FOR**

*Children sing about how God stops all their fears, with fun finger motions and easy words—set to the tune of 'The farmer's in his den'.*

**SCRIPTURE**

Isaiah 41:13

## Sing it!

**When Halloween is here,**
*(hands up, fingers open, then closed)*

**And scary things appear,**
*(hands up, fingers open, then closed to a neighbour)*

**Oh, God Almighty**
*(hands up, fingers open, then closed)*

**STOPS all my fear!**
*(on 'STOPS', hold hands straight out, as if to say, 'Stop!')*


**When scary things appear,**
*(hands up, fingers open, then closed)*

**God is always near,**
*(hands up, fingers open, then closed to a neighbour)*

**Oh, God Almighty**
*(hands up, fingers open, then closed)*

**STOPS all my fear!**
*(On 'STOPS', hold hands straight out, as if to say, 'Stop!')*

# Reverse the curse

*Children will go trick-or-treating—in reverse!*

**SCRIPTURE**

John 3:16

**WHAT YOU'LL NEED**

- sweets
- invitations to your church services or a mission event
- Bibles to give away (optional)

## The experience

This Halloween, send your children out with adult chaperones to your church's neighbourhood to go trick-or-treating in reverse. (Check with the parents first that they are happy to let their children do this.) Give the children sweets and invitations to hand out to residents when they knock on doors. Instead of saying, 'Trick-or-treat!' ask them to say, 'Here's a treat: Jesus loves you!' (It would be worth preparing the children for the occasional negative response.)

As a bonus, in the weeks leading up to Halloween, take up a special collection among your church members so you can offer Bibles to people as well.

## DID YOU KNOW...?

Pumpkins are thought to have originated in North America. Seeds dating from between 7000 and 5500 BC were found in Mexico.

## DID YOU KNOW...?

The word 'pumpkin' comes from the Greek 'pepōn', which means 'large melon'. The French changed it to 'pompon', which the British changed to 'pumpion', and later American colonists finally settled on 'pumpkin'.

# REMEMBRANCE Day

Remembrance is an important theme in the Bible. The Israelites set up stones of remembrance after crossing the River Jordan. At the Last Supper, Jesus asked his disciples to continue to eat bread and drink from the cup to remember his sacrifice. Remembrance Day is a time set aside for remembering, too. The activities in this section help children to reflect on and honour those who have died to protect them—including Jesus.

# Stones of remembrance

**BEST Primary Age FOR**

*Children set up a stone memorial as a way to thank Jesus and others for their sacrifices.*

## SCRIPTURE

Joshua 4:1–8; John 15:13

## WHAT YOU'LL NEED

- Bible
- large rock
- tarpaulin or old rug
- fine-tip permanent markers (watch that younger children don't get pen on their clothes)
- stones

## The experience

Before the children arrive, put a tarpaulin or old rug on the floor in the corner of the room and write 'People who've died for us' on the large rock. Set the rock out of sight.

SAY: **On Remembrance Day, we remember the sacrifices of those who died protecting our country and all those who have died in war.**

**Think silently about someone who made a sacrifice for you. Maybe it's something small, like letting you have the last brownie. Or maybe it's something bigger, like a friend who gave you their favourite toy.**

As the children think, distribute a stone and pen to each child.

**Tip** If stones are too hard to find, build a rock wall instead by cutting small stone shapes out of sugar paper and getting the children to Blu-Tack® them to the wall. Set the large stone in front of the wall.

SAY: **In the Bible, people sometimes used a pile of stones to remember something special. In Joshua 3–4, God helped the Israelites to get across the River Jordan. To remember what God did for them, the Israelites made a pile of twelve stones by the river. Let's remember the sacrifices you thought of just now the same way. Write or draw about the sacrifice someone made for you on your stone. When you've finished, you can come up and set the stone on the tarpaulin.**

After the children have set their stones on the tarpaulin, read John 15:13. Bring out the large rock and set it in front of the pile of stones.

SAY: **There's one sacrifice that Jesus said was the greatest of all—giving up your life for someone else. This big rock helps us remember that great sacrifice that many men and women have made to keep our country safe. And it helps us remember that Jesus also gave his life for us.**

ASK: **What are some things you can do to remember what soldiers have done for you?**

- **What are some things you can do to remember what Jesus has done for you?**

SAY: **One thing you can do is keep adding to the rock pile. Any time someone makes a sacrifice for you or God does something really amazing in your life, you can write it on a stone and add it to our pile here.**

Place blank stones by the pile so children can add to it any time. Bring the pile out at every session for the next few weeks.

# Memory bracelets

*Children make bracelets to wear as a reminder of loved ones who have died.*

## SCRIPTURE

Matthew 5:4

## WHAT YOU'LL NEED

- Bible
- snap-on bracelets (available online; also known as slap bracelets)
- fine-tip permanent markers (watch that younger children don't get pen on their clothes)
- assorted foam stickers

## The experience

SAY: **Remembrance Day is a day for remembering the men and women who died while serving in our armed forces. We can remember that even though those people gave their lives, their sacrifice has helped keep our country safe.**

ASK: **Tell us about a person you know who served in the armed forces.** (If children don't know anyone, share a story about someone you know.)

- **What kinds of sacrifices did that person have to make to serve our country?**

SAY: **Remembrance Day can also be a time when people remember loved ones who have died, even if they didn't serve in the armed forces.**

ASK: **Talk about someone in your family who has died.** (Bear in mind that some children may become upset remembering loved ones who have died, so be ready to comfort them.)

- **What's your favourite memory of that person?**

- **Why do you think it's important to** remember special things about people who have died?

SAY: **Losing people we love makes us very sad, but the Bible says that God will comfort us.** Read Matthew 5:4. **Also, we can keep the memories of our loved ones alive. We can do this by making a bracelet in memory of that person.**

Hand out snap-on bracelets and markers. Encourage the children to write the name of a person they shared about and 'You are in my heart!' on one side of the bracelet.

They can then add foam stickers to the other side of the bracelet and decorate it with the marker pens.

Encourage the children to keep and wear their bracelets in memory of the special people in their lives who've died. Tell them that when they see their bracelets, they can remember to thank God for their lost loved ones.

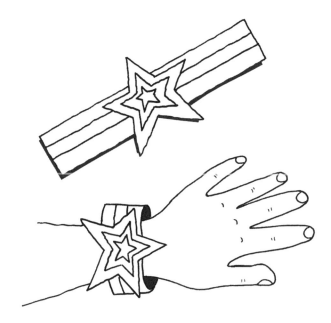

BEST
Primary Age
FOR

# Movement memory

*Children are challenged to use their brains in this engaging game.*

**SCRIPTURE**

Deuteronomy 4:9

**WHAT YOU'LL NEED**

• Bible

## The experience

Stand in a large circle of ten or more.

SAY: **Be careful! Watch closely so you don't forget the things your eyes have seen. Don't let them slip from your heart—as long as you live!**

Say your full name, first and last, while doing some kind of unique movement. For example, you could say your name while lifting your right leg and hitting your knee with your hand for every syllable.

SAY: **Now, let's teach these to our children, and to their children after them.** Have the person to your right repeat your name and action, then say his or her full name and add one unique action. Continue around the circle, with each child repeating the name and action of everyone before them, then adding their own name and action.

After going all around the circle, ASK:

• **What was easy or hard about remembering everyone's name and action?**

• **What kinds of things do you think it's important to remember about loved ones?**

Read aloud Deuteronomy 4:9.

SAY: **This scripture is Moses talking to the people of Israel, asking them to follow the ten commandments that God had given him. He was urging the people never to forget what they'd seen, and to teach their children and their children's children all about God. It was very important for them to remember what Moses told them. In the same spirit, Remembrance Day is a time for us to remember those who've fought and died for our country and our freedoms. We remember why people are willing to die for other people's freedoms.**

Ask the children to talk about any friends or family members they have serving in the armed forces or who have died while serving. Then pray, thanking God for the men and women who have given their lives for our freedom.

Extra-special
FACT

DID YOU KNOW...?

Remembrance Day is observed on 11 November in most countries to remember the end of World War I hostilities on that date in 1918, 'at the 11th hour of the 11th day of the 11th month'.

 Snack

# Pepper poppies

BEST
All Ages
FOR

*Children celebrate Remembrance Day with pepper poppies.*

**SCRIPTURE**

Isaiah 1:17

**WHAT YOU'LL NEED**

- Bible
- red peppers (or strawberries), sliced into segments
- sliced black olives (or blueberries)
- thin slices of cucumber (or liquorice)
- paper plates

## The experience

Ask the children to wash their hands, then give each child a paper plate and help them arrange their ingredients into a poppy shape, with the pepper/strawberries as petals around a centre made of olives/blueberries, and the cucumber/liquorice as a stem.

SAY: **This week, we're celebrating Remembrance Day. This is when we remember people who have died in war, both those who have fought as soldiers and civilians caught up in the conflict.**

ASK: **Do you know anyone who has served in the armed forces?**

Read Isaiah 1:17.

SAY: **This is something we can all do, but today we want to say a special thank you to those who have defended our country. Poppies are a symbol of those who died fighting to keep others safe.**

SAY: **I'm going to pray before our snack. When I pause, you can say the name of anyone you know who has served or is serving our country so that we can thank God for that person.**

PRAY: **Dear God, we thank you for keeping our country safe. We thank you for the people who have served in the armed forces to defend our country, some even giving the ultimate sacrifice of their lives. We thank you for...** *(pause to let the children fill in names)***. And we thank you that you gave your life for us on the cross. In Jesus' name, Amen**

# Remembered

 BEST All Ages FOR

*In this sketch, a boy remembers fallen heroes.*

**SCRIPTURE**

Deuteronomy 4:9

**PROPS**

- room divider (e.g. sheet hung between poles)
- bouquet of flowers

**CAST**

- Soldier One
- Soldier Two
- Boy

**BEHIND THE SCENES**

The stage can be divided by either a free-standing room divider or a sheet hung between two poles. Visually, it should look as though the boy is going to a memorial wall of some kind, and the soldiers are behind it—but the audience can see both the boy and the soldiers. The soldiers can be dressed in military uniforms, but this isn't necessary.

## Action!

➡ *Soldier One moves to one side of the divider. Soldier Two enters behind Soldier One and they salute each other.*

### SOLDIER ONE

You made it back, Private. Happy to see you're still in one piece.

### SOLDIER TWO

Quite a battle out there, sir. Enemy attacked in the dead of night. We weren't expecting it.

### SOLDIER ONE

You were trained for this. Good work out there, soldier.

### SOLDIER TWO

Thank you, sir. *(Sighs)*

### SOLDIER ONE

Something on your mind?

### SOLDIER TWO

Sometimes I just wonder what we're doing this for, sir.

### SOLDIER ONE

We're fighting the enemy, preserving the greater good.

### SOLDIER TWO

But for what, sir? No one seems to remember that we're here. They go on with their lives back home and we're over here—fighting this war.

### SOLDIER ONE

Well, you're right about that, Private— but we don't focus on that. We do our best.

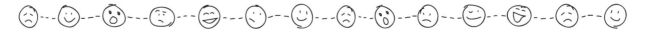

## SOLDIER TWO

Our best. *(Sighs)* **Yes, sir.**

➡ *Just then, a boy enters. He is carrying a bouquet of flowers. He kneels down facing the divider as if he's visiting a memorial wall. He lays the flowers on the floor and runs his hand along the divider.*

## BOY

Private Harold Taylor.

## SOLDIER TWO

Did you hear that, sir?

## SOLDIER ONE

What's that, Private?

## SOLDIER TWO

Someone just said my name, sir.

## BOY

Private Taylor, my daddy says you're a hero.

## SOLDIER TWO

Me? A hero?

## BOY

He says you were my great-grandpa, and you fought in a terrible war. He says you saved lots of people. They gave you a Victoria Cross. It's a medal, and it means you were really brave.

## SOLDIER TWO

A Victoria Cross? Me?

## BOY

Daddy told me it's Remembrance Day, and he brought us to visit you. He makes sure we always remember what you did for us and for our country, because if it weren't for people like you, we might not be able to do things like worship God in church on Sunday.

➡ *Soldier Two smiles warmly.*

## BOY

So, these flowers are for you—to say 'thanks', and to tell you that even though I never got to meet you, I'll never forget you. I'm going to tell my own kids all about you one day. *(Pauses, then whispers)* You're my hero, Great-Grandpa.

➡ *Soldier Two turns back to Soldier One.*

## SOLDIER ONE

Sometimes, soldier, they do remember.

# We remember

BEST Preschool FOR

*Children remember and thank those who gave their lives for freedom with a song set to the tune of 'Oh, my darlin' Clementine'.*

**SCRIPTURE**

Deuteronomy 4:9

## Sing it!

**We remember, we remember,**

*(point to your head, as if thinking)*

**We remember on this day**

*(hold up one index finger)*

**That you fought for**

*(on 'fought for', hit fist into palm twice)*

**All our freedom,**

*(hold hands out to sides, palms up)*

**We remember on this day.**

*(point to your head, as if thinking)*

**All the soldiers, all the soldiers,**

*(march on the spot)*

**We remember on this day**

*(hold up one index finger)*

**That you died for**

*(On 'died for', hit fist into palm twice)*

**All our freedom,**

*(hold hands out to sides, palms up)*

**We remember on this day.**

*(point to your head, as if thinking)*

## Extra-special FACTS

### DID YOU KNOW...?

Red poppies are recognised as the Remembrance Day flower, inspired by a World War I poem by John McCrae, 'In Flanders Fields'.

### DID YOU KNOW...?

The American equivalent of Remembrance Day is Memorial Day, held on the last Monday in May. The first Memorial Day took place on 30 May 1868. General James Garfield made a speech at Arlington National Cemetery, after which 5000 participants placed flowers on the graves of more than 20,000 Union and Confederate soldiers buried there.

# We will not forget

*Children make a memorial banner to honour those who've lost their lives for our country.*

### SCRIPTURE

Luke 22:19

### WHAT YOU'LL NEED

- large white bedsheet
- black buttons
- green ribbon
- red felt or other red material
- scissors
- black, red and green fabric pens
- craft glue
- spreaders

## The experience

Before the session, visit a local war memorial and note down some of the names of people who died in World War I and World War II. If you know of local people who have been killed serving in more recent conflicts, add their names to the list.

SAY: **Remembrance Day is about remembering the people who have died for us and for our country. The first person who ever died just for you was Jesus. Just before he died, Jesus served his disciples a final meal and told them to continue the practice of serving a special meal in his memory. He told them, 'Do this in remembrance of me' (Luke 22:19). Let's remember the people who have died for our country with a special banner.**

**1.** Ask one child to write the words 'We will not forget' near the bottom of the sheet in large letters using fabric pens. Leave space underneath the words for the children to sign their names at the end of the activity.

**2.** Encourage the children to create poppies on the rest of the sheet, using black buttons for the centre, green ribbon for the stalk and red fabric for the petals. These can be stuck on with craft glue. The children can also use the fabric pens to draw some poppies.

**3.** Help the children to write among the poppies the names of local people who died serving their country.

**4.** Ask the children to sign their first name under the words 'We will not forget', to show their thanks for the sacrifice.

**5.** Put the banner on display in your church so that people can view it at your church's Remembrance Sunday service.

# Christmas

*Merry Christmas*

For lots of people, Christmas is associated with shopping, presents, stress, busyness and Santa. But the Bible introduces a simple, humble first Christmas centred around a baby in a manger. This baby, Jesus, came from heaven as the Saviour of the world. Amid the hubbub that Christmas encompasses today, you can bring your children back to the humble beginnings of Christmas and point them to Jesus with these activities.

# Eyes on Jesus

BEST Primary Age FOR

*Children search for a partner as they experience how the wise men searched for Jesus.*

**SCRIPTURE**

Matthew 2:8–12

**WHAT YOU'LL NEED**

• Bible

## The experience

Ask the children to stand in a circle. You'll need an even number of children in the circle, so decide whether or not to participate based on how many children you have.

SAY: **It's Christmas, and we're celebrating Jesus' birth. Today we're learning about how the wise men searched to find baby Jesus. Let's experience what it's like to search for someone right now.**

SAY: **You're going to close your eyes. When I say, 'Search!' open your eyes, look out across the circle and try to lock eyes with someone.** Let the children practise.

SAY: **Now let's play. When I tell you to search, if the person you look at is looking back at you, run to the centre of the circle and celebrate finding each other with a high five; then move outside the circle as a pair. If you're looking at someone who's looking at someone else, then stay in our circle for another round and close your eyes again.**

Repeat until all the children are in pairs.

Then ask them to discuss the following questions with their partners.

ASK: **Describe what it was like trying to lock eyes with a partner.**

• **Talk about a time you looked really hard for something—and then you found it.**

SAY: **To lock eyes with someone, you had to focus, act quickly and pay attention. Let's see what the wise men did to 'lock eyes' with baby Jesus.**

Read aloud Matthew 2:8–12.

ASK: **How were the wise men focused on baby Jesus?**

SAY: **The wise men searched for baby Jesus. They followed the star in the east to find him. When the wise men found Jesus, they were filled with joy. They knelt down in front of him and worshipped him.**

ASK: **At Christmas, what kinds of things take your attention away from Jesus?**

• **Why do you think shops and adverts seem to focus on everything *except* Jesus?**

• **What are ways you can stay focused on Jesus at Christmas?**

SAY: **This Christmas we can celebrate the joy of baby Jesus, too. We can keep our focus on him.**

PRAY: **Dear God, thank you for sending Jesus. Help us keep our eyes on him—today and every day. In Jesus' name, Amen**

Please note that children with autism spectrum disorders may find this activity difficult.

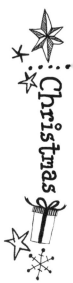

# Mini manger

*Children create a crafty mini nativity that makes a delightful decoration.*

## SCRIPTURE

Luke 2:6–7

## WHAT YOU'LL NEED

- Bible
- wooden dolly pegs
- Blu-Tack® or similar
- mini wooden shaker pegs or 3 cm wooden dowel pins
- squares of card, big enough for the napkin ring and pegs to stand on
- assorted wool

- PVA glue and spreaders
- scissors
- hot-glue gun (adult use only)
- wooden napkin rings (or pieces of kitchen towel tube)
- straw or shredded yellow paper

## The experience

Read aloud Luke 2:6–7.

ASK: **What do you think that first Christmas looked like?**

• **What are your favourite ways to decorate your house for Christmas?**

SAY: **The way people decorate for Christmas is often a lot fancier than the inside of a barn, which is where Jesus was born. We're going to make simple Christmas decorations today that show what happened in the verses we read.**

**1.** Give each child two dolly pegs, one mini shaker peg or dowel pin (watch that younger children don't put these in their mouths), a blob of Blu-Tack® and one napkin

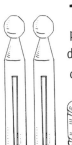

ring. Get the children to stick the Blu-Tack® to the bottom of one of the round dolly pegs to make it taller. This peg is Joseph. The other peg is Mary, and the shaker peg is baby Jesus.

**2.** Using PVA glue, stick the end of a piece of wool to the bottom of each dolly peg, then ask the children to wrap each peg with the wool, leaving the heads exposed. Do the same with the shaker peg.

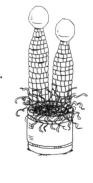

**3.** With a hot-glue gun, glue the Mary and Joseph pegs together and then glue them to the outside of the napkin ring so they are all level at the bottom. Glue the bottom of the decoration to the square of card.

**4.** Get the children to cut the straw into small pieces and stuff the napkin ring with it; or use shredded paper.

**5.** Glue the shaker peg Jesus to the top of the straw inside the napkin ring. The children now have their very own mini manger scene! (Remind the children to keep the decorations out of reach of younger siblings, as the mini shaker peg could be a choking hazard.)

# Poinsettia Christmas trees

*As children press poinsettia leaves into the shape of Christmas trees, they'll learn how Christmas trees can point us to Jesus.*

## SCRIPTURE

Matthew 2:1–2

## WHAT YOU'LL NEED

- Bible
- poinsettia plants
- A4 sheets of paper
- glue
- silver glitter glue

## The experience

Show the children a poinsettia plant. Point out the star shape of each flower.

SAY: **Poinsettias are often bought at Christmas because they're great winter plants, and the star shape of the flower reminds us of the first Christmas star.**

Read aloud Matthew 2:1–2.

ASK: **What are other places you see stars around Christmas?**

SAY: **Another place we see the Christmas star is on a Christmas tree. There's a story from hundreds of years ago that tells of a Christian named Martin Luther. He went for a walk in the woods around Christmas and noticed how the snow shimmered on the branches of the evergreen trees. It reminded him of a shining star, pointing us to heaven. So he took a tree home and decorated it for Christmas.**

**Let's use poinsettias and Christmas trees to make a fun craft that points us to Jesus.**

Give each child a sheet of paper. Get the children to pick leaves and petals off the poinsettia and arrange them in the shape of a Christmas tree on the paper. Then ask them to glue the leaves on to the paper.

Let the children decorate their creations with silver glitter glue to make the branches shimmer the way Martin Luther observed.

ASK: **What can we do this Christmas to stay focused on Jesus?**

Get the children to hold up their crafts.

SAY: **Our Christmas trees help us remember Jesus in another way, too. They're pointy at the top, like an arrow pointing to heaven. This Christmas, make sure your celebrations all point to Jesus!**

## Game

# Count your chickens

BEST
All Ages
FOR

*Animal sounds abound in this fun Christmas game!*

**WHAT YOU'LL NEED**

• no supplies needed

## The experience

In a large group, number the children one to five, and ask them to remember their numbers.

SAY: **Baby Jesus was born in a stable. A stable is a place where animals eat and sleep. However, the animals have all escaped from our stable!** Get the children to spread out around the room. Assign animals to the numbers. For example, all of the number ones are cows, the twos are horses, the threes are chickens and so on. Choose animals that make distinctive sounds. Explain that the children must get on all fours, close their eyes and locate their group just by listening to and making the animal sounds.

SAY: **Ready? Go!** Allow time for all the children to find their groups.

When the 'animals' are all grouped together, SAY: **Now, I don't know if there were actually cows and chickens in the stable where Jesus was born, but I do know that angels appeared nearby, to tell shepherds to go and visit Jesus. What a great way to celebrate a birthday!**

Have 'animal' groups discuss the following. ASK:
• **How do you celebrate your birthday?**
• **What are some ways you celebrate Jesus' birthday?**
• **Why is it important to celebrate Jesus' birth?**

Extra-special
**FACT**

DID YOU KNOW...?

The first artificial Christmas trees were made in Germany. They were made of goose feathers that had been dyed green.

# Good news angel

 BEST All Ages FOR

*This snack comes bearing good news that will bring great joy to all people!*

## SCRIPTURE

Luke 2:8–14

 ALLERGY ALERT *see p. 7*

## WHAT YOU'LL NEED

- Bible
- large, round waffles (or scotch pancakes or crumpets)
- oven or toaster
- small round biscuits
- raisins or chocolate chips
- banana slices (cut up at the last minute so they don't go brown)
- jelly orange slices
- icing sugar in a bowl
- syrup or chocolate sauce
- large paper plates
- napkins
- plastic knives
- forks and spoons
- condiment cups for the syrup or chocolate sauce

## The experience

Heat the waffles. <u>SAY:</u> **It's Christmas, and we're celebrating the birth of Jesus.**

<u>ASK:</u> **What's something you know about Christmas?**

• **How did you learn those things?**

<u>SAY:</u> **Let's see how people first found out Jesus was born.** Read aloud Luke 2:8–12. **Let's make angels appear right now to remind us of the good news that Jesus was born.**

**1.** Ask the children to wash their hands. Set out the snack supplies.

**2.** Get the children to place the large round waffle on the plate and carefully cut a thin segment from each side to form two wings.

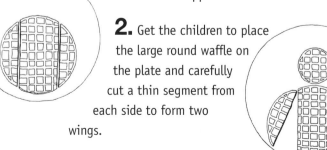

**3.** Adjust the wings so there's a small space between each wing and the angel's body.

**4.** Place the small biscuit above the body on the plate to make the head.

**5.** Add raisins or chocolate chips for eyes and a jelly orange slice for a mouth.

**6.** Use a banana slice for a halo.

**7.** Let the children dust the angel with icing sugar.

**8.** Hand out forks. Serve with an individual cup of syrup or chocolate sauce for dunking.

After the children have made their angels, get them to make the orange slice mouths move as you read Luke 2:13–14.

<u>ASK:</u> **Describe a time when something amazing happened to you. Who did you tell about it?**

• **What can you do to spread the good news of Jesus like the angels did?**

<u>SAY:</u> **The angels delivered some pretty amazing news to the shepherds. Later, the shepherds passed on the news, too! We can continue passing on the good news of the great joy of Jesus' birth.**

# Find-and-eat Christmas story

*With this edible nativity, children experience the Christmas story in a delicious way!*

## SCRIPTURE

Luke 2:1–20; Matthew 2:1–11

## WHAT YOU'LL NEED

- Bible
- sandwich bags
- 9 bowls
- white chocolate buttons
- mini marshmallows
- Pom-Bear® snacks or similar
- gummy bears or similar
- bitesize Shredded Wheat®
- gold chocolate coins
- Twiglets® or similar
- raisins
- animal biscuits
- plates

## The experience

Place each ingredient in a bowl and set up an assembly line for the children to make their snacks. Get the children to wash their hands.

SAY: **You're going to create your snack today by placing one of each item in your bag. When you get to the gummy bears and Pom-Bears®, take three of each of those.**

Let the children go through the assembly line, each putting the following in a bag:

1 white chocolate button

1 mini marshmallow

1 bitesize Shredded Wheat®

1 gold chocolate coin

1 Twiglet®

1 raisin

1 animal biscuit

3 Pom-Bears®

3 different-coloured gummy bears

Monitor the line, helping the children to remember to take extra gummy bears and Pom-Bears®.

Distribute plates. Open your Bible to Luke 2:1–20.

SAY: **It's Christmas, and we're celebrating Jesus' birth. Let's experience the true story of how Jesus was born with our tasty treats. As I tell the Christmas story, find the ingredient I show you in your 'find-and-eat treat' and set it on your plate.**

Hold up a gummy bear, and let the children find one of theirs. **A long time ago, there was a young girl named Mary, who was visited by an angel.** Hold up the white chocolate button and let the children find their 'angel'. **The angel told Mary that she was going to have a baby, and that the baby would be named Jesus.**

**Mary was engaged to a man named Joseph.** Hold up a second gummy bear, and let the children find theirs. **Joseph and Mary had to travel a long way to the town of Bethlehem.** Get the children to make the two gummy bears 'walk'.

**When Joseph and Mary arrived in Bethlehem, there was no place for them to stay. Finally an innkeeper told Joseph that they could stay in his stable with the animals.** Hold up an animal biscuit, and let the children find theirs. **Mary and Joseph rested among the animals.** Let the children act out the scene with their gummy bears and animal biscuit. **Then Mary had her baby.** Let the children find the

third gummy bear. **They wrapped Jesus in a blanket and put him in a manger.** Let the children find the Shredded Wheat® and place their third gummy bear on it.

**Nearby in the hills some shepherds tending flocks of sheep noticed a bright light in the sky.** Let the children find the mini marshmallow. **An angel appeared and told them that Jesus, the Son of God, was born.** Encourage the children to make the white chocolate button hover over the marshmallow. **The shepherds went to Bethlehem to see the baby Jesus.** Get the children to lead their marshmallow to the manger.

**Some time later, far away, three wise men saw a bright star in the sky.** Let the children find their three Pom-Bears®. **The wise men followed the star to see what they could find. The bright star led them to Jesus.** Get the children to 'walk' the Pom-Bears® to the manger.

The wise men knelt down and worshipped the baby Jesus. They gave Jesus presents of gold, frankincense and myrrh.** Get the children to set their gold chocolate coin, Twiglet® and raisin between the Pom-Bears® and the Shredded Wheat®.

Let the children arrange their snack however they like to depict the nativity scene. Then let them eat it as you discuss the following questions.

<u>ASK:</u> **What was your favourite part of our snack?**

• **What is sweet to you about Christmas?**

<u>SAY:</u> **Mary and Joseph can teach us about obeying God no matter what. The angels and shepherds show us how to spread the good news. And the wise men show us how to worship Jesus. This Christmas, look for ways to obey, talk about and worship Jesus.**

BEST
All Ages
FOR

# The Son that God gave

An interactive sketch where children experience how Jesus was sent to earth to 'untangle' our sins—and how he is a light of hope in the darkness of the world.

### SCRIPTURE

Luke 2:1–20

### PROPS

- 3 strings of Christmas lights
- extension lead, with one end plugged into a wall socket (check it isn't a trip hazard). The lead needs to have at least three sockets.

### CAST

- Narrator
- 3 group leaders

### BEHIND THE SCENES

Plug one end of the extension lead into a socket. Get the audience to form three groups, each led by a group leader and holding a string of Christmas lights. (Test the lights beforehand to make sure they are in good working condition.) Ensure the group leaders are briefed to weave in and out gently and carefully so that the strings of lights do not get tugged or damaged. If you have a large audience, create more groups (with additional group leaders and strings of Christmas lights).

# Action!

➡ *The narrator begins centre stage. He or she asks the audience to form three separate groups. Get the groups to sit and then hand each a string of Christmas lights. Ask the groups to unroll the lights so everyone in the group is holding on to a part of the strand.*

## NARRATOR

**This is the Son that God gave.**

➡ *Group One stands, holding its string of lights with the group leader at the front of the line.*

## NARRATOR

**Mary is the mum, who had the Son God gave.**

➡ *Group Two stands, holding its string of lights with the group leader at the front of the line.*

## NARRATOR

**Joseph is the dad, who married the mum, who had the Son that God gave.**

➡ *Group Three stands, holding its string of lights with the group leader at the front of the line. All three groups, led by the group leaders, start to cross each other's lines, ducking and weaving in and out, beginning to tangle up the lines and strings of Christmas lights. The group leaders (and their groups) should stop moving at the end of each of the narrator's sentences.*

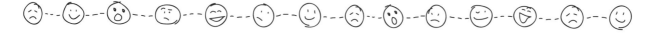

## NARRATOR

This is the town, where Joseph was from, who is also the dad, who married the mum, who had the Son that God gave.

➡ *All three groups stop moving when the narrator pauses. The group leaders begin moving again when the narrator starts speaking. This happens on every one of the narrator's sentences.*

## NARRATOR

This is the inn, the inn in the town, where Joseph was from, who's also the dad, who married the mum, who had the Son that God gave.

➡ *Narrator pauses, groups stop, then groups begin again on narrator's next sentence.*

## NARRATOR

There was a man who ran the inn, the inn in the town, where Joseph was from, who's also the dad, who married the mum, who had the Son that God gave.

➡ *Narrator pauses, groups stop, then groups begin again on narrator's next sentence.*

## NARRATOR

This is the barn, a stable of sorts, owned by the man who ran the inn. Remember the inn? The inn in the town, where Joseph was from, who's also the dad, who married the mum, who had the Son that God gave.

➡ *Narrator pauses, groups stop, then groups begin again on narrator's next sentence.*

## NARRATOR

This is the cow that mooed in the barn, a stable of sorts, owned by the man who ran the inn. Remember the inn? The inn in the town, where Joseph was from, who's also the dad, who married the mum, who had the Son that God gave.

➡ *Pause for a moment, and get the children to look around at their tangled mess. The group leaders remain still.*

## NARRATOR

The reason that God sent Jesus to earth was not because he was bored.
The reason that God sent Jesus to earth was because earth needed a Lord. *(Pauses)*
So... in the barn, a baby was born!

## GROUP LEADERS

*(To their groups)* **Repeat after me, 'Jesus was born!'**

## AUDIENCE/LEADERS/ NARRATOR

**Jesus was born! Jesus was born!**

➡ *When the narrator continues, group leaders and children, without letting go of their Christmas lights, start to unravel and untangle their strings carefully to get back to their groups on the narrator's cue.*

## NARRATOR

**Time to untangle, from head to toe! Ready? Steady? Here we go! Jesus was born! Next to the cow! Born in the barn! Remember the barn? A stable of sorts, owned by the man. Remember the man? He ran the inn. Remember the inn? The inn in the town, where Joseph was from, who's also the dad, who married the mum, who had the Son that God gave.**

➡ *Once the groups are untangled, the group leaders should plug their Christmas lights into the extension lead (but don't switch the plug on at the wall yet). If possible, turn out all the lights in the room.*

## NARRATOR

**The people on earth looked like you did just now—**
**A bewildered, tangled-up jumble.**
**But Jesus, God's Son, in swaddling cloth curled,**
**As angels and shepherds and praises all swirled...**
**This baby would be the light of the world**
*(switch on the lights)*
**And save us all from our sins.**

BEST
Preschool
FOR

# Jesus, our saviour

*A song about Jesus' birth, sung to the tune of 'Pop goes the weasel'.*

**SCRIPTURE**

Luke 2:1–20

## Sing it!

**All the way to Bethlehem,**

*(raise right arm to make one side of a house shape)*

**To end up in a stable,**

*(raise left arm to complete the house shape)*

**He was born on Christmas Day,**

*(bring hands down, palms up)*

**Jesus, our saviour!**

*(raise hands over heads, palms up)*

**Mary and Joseph,**

*(wave right hand and keep it up)*

**Shepherds and angels,**

*(wave left hand and keep it up)*

**They all worshipped God's Son,**

*(bring hands down, palms up)*

**Jesus, our saviour!**

*(raise hands over heads, palms up)*

JUST FOR FUN...

What did Adam say on 24 December?

'It's Christmas, Eve!'

# Welcome home

*Jesus made the earth his home, and children can help make their town a welcoming home for new residents.*

### SCRIPTURE

John 1:14

### WHAT YOU'LL NEED

- list of contact information for local council offices, post offices, libraries and so on
- felt-tip pens
- whiteboard and pens
- address labels, with information about your church's Christmas services printed on them
- C5-size envelopes (or bigger if your church brochure is bigger)
- church brochures
- local business vouchers (optional)

## The experience

Prepare ahead by contacting local estate agents to get an idea of how many people move to your area from out of town each month. Print that many copies of contact details for important places like council offices, post offices, libraries and supermarkets. Leave room at the bottom of the page. Also print information about your Christmas services on address labels.

With the children, read John 1:14.

SAY: **Jesus came to earth in a stable, with cloths for blankets and shepherds as the welcoming committee. Even though a barn isn't the cosiest place to call home, he had people around to make his home on earth welcoming.**

**Let's do the same thing for new people in our town. To welcome them, we'll make some welcome packs.**

First, ask the children to vote for their favourite restaurants, parks and other places to go. Write the winning two votes of each category on a whiteboard. Distribute copies of the contact details sheet and help the children to write at the bottom, 'We also recommend:' with the names of places that won the most votes.

Then get the children to decorate the envelopes with phrases such as 'Welcome to our town!' or 'Get to know your new home!' They can also decorate the envelopes with wreaths, Christmas trees, ornaments, stars and other Christmas pictures. Fill the envelopes with one contact details sheet and one church brochure per envelope. Stick the address labels with information about your church's Christmas services on to the church brochures.

You could also contact local businesses such as restaurants, hairdressers and supermarkets to see if they can offer any money-off vouchers to put in the packs.

Ask the children to hold the envelopes and pray for the people who'll receive them.

Ask estate agents and schools to keep the packs to hand out to new residents, or attach them to community bulletin boards.

BEST
Primary Age
FOR

# Treasure jars

## The experience

Read Luke 2:19.

SAY: **A lot of mums treasure their new babies in the same way as Mary. Let's give new mums a special gift by making them treasure jars.**

Let each child choose a clean jar to decorate with colourful sticky-back plastic. Ask the children to write 'Treasure Jar' on an address label and stick it on the jar. They can then add baby-themed stickers to the sticky-back plastic for extra decoration. Older children could add Luke 2:11–12 or another message about Jesus' birth.

Get the children to start each jar off with treasuring thoughts written on an index card by completing sentences such as:

'My wish for you is…'

'You are blessed because…'

'Your life is special because…'

'I hope you feel…'

Then fill each jar with blank index cards and a pen, placing the pre-written cards on top.

Contact your local hospital and ask about placing the jars where new mums can each take one to record their thoughts and memories of their babies' first days. If the hospital is unwilling, give them to your church's mums-and-toddlers group to hand out to new mums.

*Children help new mothers treasure their babies, just as Mary did.*

**SCRIPTURE**

Luke 2:19

**WHAT YOU'LL NEED**

- Bible
- clean jars
- rolls of patterned sticky-back plastic (available online)
- address labels
- baby-themed stickers
- index cards
- felt-tip pens
- pens small enough to fit into jars

Extra-special
**FACT**

DID YOU KNOW…?

If you received every present in the song 'The twelve days of Christmas', you'd have a total of 364 presents!

# Handouts

# Father's Day symbols

# Peek-a-boo for dad symbols

# Treasure ties

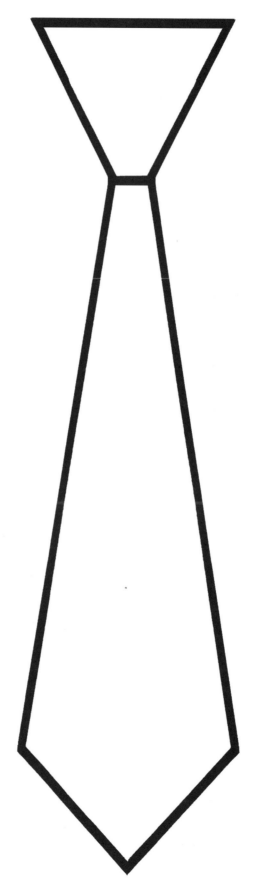

# Optical illusion

# Index

# ALSO FROM BRF

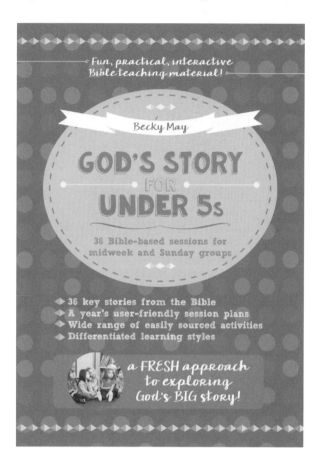

Let's share God's big story! Use as a year-long weekly programme or dip in and out to highlight individual stories at key times of year and supplement other activities. Varied storytelling methods enable children to engage with God's big story in different ways, with a range of activities to illustrate and explore the story, catering for different learning preferences and using materials that most children's groups will already have to hand.

**God's Story for Under 5s**

978 0 85746 381 4 £12.99

**God's Story for 5–7s**

978 0 85746 425 5 £12.99

**God's Story for 7–11s**

978 0 85746 426 2 £12.99

brfonline.org.uk

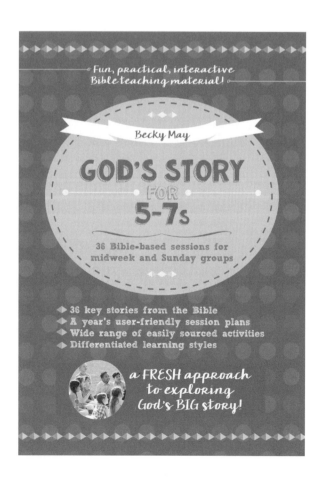

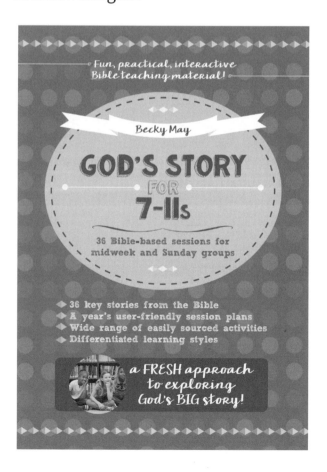

If only you could be sure that every craft you planned for your children's ministry would be a winner… Now you can be certain of success with over 100 tried-and-tested crafts, submitted by children's workers like you, and used with real children in real churches. Structured into three sections of crafts for younger and older primary ages and for all ages together, *The Big Book of Bible Crafts* is a lifesaver for Sunday school, midweek groups and holiday clubs.

**The Big Book of Bible Crafts**
Edited by Laurie Copley
978 0 85746 495 8  £11.99

brfonline.org.uk